D✛GΜA

Other books by
Kevin Smith

Screenplays:

Clerks & Chasing Amy

Graphic Novels:

Daredevil: Guardian Devil

Jay and Silent Bob: Chasing Dogma

D✪GMA

A Screenplay by

Kevin Smith

Grove Press
New York

Published simultaneously in Canada

Printed in the United States of America

FIRST EDITION

Library of Congress Catalog Card Number 99-76041

ISBN 0-8021-3679-6

Grove Press
841 Broadway
New York, NY 10003

99 00 01 02   10 9 8 7 6 5 4 3 2 1

DEDICATION

This screenplay, this movie, and all that I am or will ever be is dedicated to God and Jesus Christ (who is also God, technically, but—not wanting Him to feel shortchanged—I'm giving him a separate shout-out as well). There are a lot of things in life that I'm not sure of (whether or not I'm a hack director, the identity of JFK's assassin, and why *Mallrats* was so thoroughly bashed are among the top ten), but what I am 100 percent on is that there is a God, and said God is responsible for creating this beautiful world we inhabit, for my blessings as husband and father, and for my career in film (which means if you object to the flicks I've done and feel I've no business working in cinema, talk to the manufacturer).

So thank you, Lord. This one—and all else—is for you.

INTRODUCTION

To tell you the truth, I'm pretty much all talked out about this flick. Whether it's the controversy about its so-called Catholic-bashing content, or what it was like to work with such great actors, or why I wrote it in the first place, I've said about all there is to say on the subject of *Dogma* over the course of the last year: except that I'm a big fan of the film. I loved it as a script, and I love it now that it's a finished flick. I know it's considered gauche to talk about how in love with your own material you are, but whenever I see or read *Dogma*, I wish it would never end. I'm usually an annoyingly modest or self-deprecating person, but I have to admit that I exempt *Dogma* from the usual self-derision I afford my other flicks, comics, etc. A lot of thought went into crafting it, a lot of heart, a lot of wit, and a lot of myself. And because of that, I feel it's my finest hour professionally.

Now, I know some will maintain that if this is my finest hour, its time to shit-can the clock, and normally I'd take it on the chin with a comment of that nature. But this time around, I'm going to have to disagree with the folks who'd slam this screenplay and tell them to take a flying leap. Because this *is* a good story, full of interesting characters, and funny, sometimes insightful dialogue. Take a shot at my directing skills if you will (for I'm not a gifted visual stylist), but I can't really take you seriously if you slam the screenplay. I just like it too much.

And I hope you like it, too.

* * *

In the end credits of the film, I thank some influences. Usually, most folks skip the credits, so I'd like to thank them again, here.

Dogma is the culmination of a lifetime's worth of disparate spiritual and satirical influences, which owes a debt to sundry storytellers and wordsmiths. These authors and instigators I humbly thank in no particular order . . .

Saint Matthew	John Milton	Robert Bolt
Saint Mark	Cervantes	Quentin Tarantino
Saint Luke	Martin Scorsese	Nikos Kazantzakis
Saint John	Alan Moore	Denys Arcand
Sam Kinison	Thomas Moore	Neil Gaiman
George Carlin	Spike Lee	Grant Morrison
Elaine Pagels	Douglas Adams	Matt Wagner

Howard, Robin, Jackie, Fred, Gary, and everyone at the *Howard Stern Show*
and Sister Theresa from eighth grade.

—Kevin Smith
October 7, 1999

Disclaimer: 1) a renunciation of any claim to or connection with; 2) a disavowal; 3) a statement made to save one's own ass.

Though it'll go without saying ten minutes or so into these proceedings, View Askew would like to state that this film is—from start to finish—a work of comedic fantasy, not to be taken seriously. To insist that any of what follows is incendiary or inflammatory is to miss our intention and pass undue judgment; and passing judgment is reserved for God and God alone (this goes for you film critics too . . . just kidding).

So please—before you think about hurting someone over this trifle of a film, remember: even God has a sense of humor. Just look at the platypus. Thank you and enjoy the show.

P.S. We sincerely apologize to all platypus enthusiasts out there who are offended by that thoughtless comment about the platypi. We at View Askew respect the noble platypus, and it is not our intention to slight these stupid creatures in anyway.

Thank you again and enjoy the show.

EXT ASBURY PARK BOARDWALK—DAY

A Jersey spring day. Beyond the wooden planks that make up the aged fun pier, the ocean waves crash onto the sandy shoreline.

An OLD MAN stares at the empty beach. His features are simple. He wears an old overcoat. His face belies good years gone by—a face that has seen more sunrises than one would suspect. He inhales the crisp, salty air and lets a small, satisfied smile cross his face.

Behind him, a large arcade with steel shuttered doors sits on the boardwalk. Three preteens skate by on Rollerblades, passing a street hockey ball between them proficiently.

The Old Man checks his watch, and looks back toward the ocean.

The skates of the three hockey-playing youths skid to a halt. We pan up to their faces—now cold and dispassionate. They look at one another and nod.

Their skates glide out of frame.

P.O.V. SKATERS—*The Old Man leans on the railing that overlooks the beach. We get closer and closer to him until . . .*

One of the skaters checks him hard into the railing. The Old Man exhales violently and falls to his knees. The two other skaters begin savagely beating on him with their hockey sticks, as he crumbles beneath them. Repeatedly their blades crash down hard on his head.

VOICE-OVER
And now, the driving force behind "Catholicism—Wow!" . . . Cardinal Glick!

The three skaters cease their beating and check the Old Man's pulse. Satisfied, they skate away, leaving his crumpled form on the boardwalk.

EXT SAINT MICHAEL'S CHURCH—DAY

A thrall of REPORTERS clap as CARDINAL GLICK takes to the podium. He strikes one as more of an agent than a man of the cloth. He removes his Wayfarers.

GLICK

Ladies and gentlemen, I stand before you a guilty, wretched
sinner. And as one of the tenets of my faith maintains that
confession is good for the soul, it behooves me to discharge
my conscience in an effort to attain the state of grace that my
office . . . indeed, my sanctity . . . demands.
(*beat*)
You're here under false pretenses. Contrary to what our P.R.
office led you to believe, Christ is *not* coming back this
morning.

The REPORTERS *laugh. Clearly, Glick's a pro.*

GLICK

We know how the majority—and the media—in this country
views the Catholic Church: they think of us as a passé,
archaic institution. They say we offer only rhetoric as
opposed to remedies for the twentieth century's moral ills.
People find the Bible obtuse—even hokey—and instead seek
the reassurance they require in the more digestible tomes of
Deborah Tannen or Deepak Chopra. And for the few that
maintain the faith, their adherence to the stringent rules and
practice of the ornate rituals which make up Catholicism can
be likened to doing the "Macarena" or the "Electric Slide" at
a wedding: easy enough steps to remember, but you're
damned if you can recall why you even bothered learning
them.
(*laughter*)
In an effort to disprove all that, the Church has appointed this
year as a time of renewal—both of faith and of style. I'm happy
to announce that—as of this month—we're dragging the old
girl into what's fast becoming the twenty-first century!

The crowd applauds. GLICK *smiles and nods as a dolly is wheeled out. Upon
it stands a large crucifix, and something else of equal size, covered in a shroud.*

GLICK

Now, what does this mean for the average church-goer? Are
we going to throw out centuries of tradition and go new age?
Heavens no—we're simply talking about a few minor

alterations to our aesthetic, really. For example, the crucifix.
While it has been a time-honored symbol of our faith, Holy
Mother Church has decided to retire this highly recognizable,
yet wholly depressing image of our Lord, Jesus Christ,
crucified. Christ didn't come to Earth to give us the "willies"!
He came to help us out! He was a booster! And it's with that
take on our Lord in mind that we've come up with a new,
more inspiring sigil.

> (*reaches for shroud*)

So, it is with great pleasure that I present you with the first of
many revamps that the "Catholicism—Wow!" campaign will
unveil over the next year. I give you . . .

GLICK *pulls a cover off an object to his right—a two-foot figure of a smiling
Christ, which offers a "thumbs up" while pointing and winking at us. The*
REPORTERS *buzz with confusion and shock.*

> GLICK

The "Buddy-Christ." Now that's not the sanctioned term
we're using for the symbol—it's just something we've been
kicking around the office. But look at it—doesn't it "pop"?
You walk into church, you see this little guy on the altar—
you feel like a million bucks. It's positive reinforcement that
the Lord's not only our God and King, but our best friend too!
He's "got your back"! He's our buddy, Christ—hence
"Buddy-Christ." Don't you love this . . .

> REPORTER 1 (*interrupting*)

Cardinal Glick—has the Church given any thought to its
position on John Doe Jersey? Will he be given the right to die
with dignity?

A louder buzz rises from the crowd. GLICK *rolls his eyes.*

> GLICK

C'mon, people. We're not here to talk about that. It's an issue
we stand firm on—euthanasia is a big no-no, just like
abortion. Murder's murder. Besides, we're here to talk about
this little guy—Buddy-Christ. Can't you just see it on chains
around people's necks?

But clearly the press is more concerned with the euthanasia issue, as they hurl queries at GLICK.

INT AIRPORT—DAY

The image of the press melee is captured on a hanging t.v. monitor, a label reading "LIVE VIA SATELLITEÓRED BANK, NEW JERSEY" *at the bottom of the screen. Pull back to reveal the busy airport terminal—particularly* LOKI, *who walks beneath the screen beside a* NUN. *She carries a donation can and looks very taken aback.*

NUN
Let me get this straight—you don't believe in God . . . because of *Alice in Wonderland*?

LOKI
Through the Looking Glass. That poem—"The Walrus and the Carpenter"? It's an indictment of organized religion. The Walrus—with his girth and good nature—obviously refers to either the Buddha, or—with his tusks—the Hindu elephant god, Lord Ganesha. This takes care of the Eastern religions. Now the Carpenter—which is an obvious reference to Jesus Christ, who was raised a carpenter's son—he represents the Western religions. And in the poem, what do they do? They dupe all the oysters into following them and proceed to shuck and devour the helpless creatures, en masse. I don't know what that says to you, but to me it says that following faiths based on these mythological figures ensures the destruction of one's inner-being.

BARTLEBY *sits amongst a row of seats by one of the arrival gates, looking at . . . a steady stream of* TRAVELERS, *exiting the gate, meeting loved ones, family.*

OC LOKI
Organized religion destroys who we are or who we can be by inhibiting our actions and decisions out of fear of an intangible parent-figure who shakes a finger at us from thousands of years ago and says, "Do it and I'll fucking spank you!"

BARTLEBY *smiles at the meet-and-greets, warmed. He digs into a bag of popcorn as* LOKI *saddles up behind him with the* NUN.

LOKI

The existentialists can keep their Kierkegaard and their Sartre. Give me Lewis Carroll any day—he knew what time it was.

NUN

The way you put it . . . I've never really thought about it like that before . . .
(*off her cassock; in self-doubt*)
What have I been doing with my life?

LOKI

My advice to you is to abandon this life of self-denial and get out there and taste it all.
(*off donation can*)
Leave this for the unenlightened. Poverty is for the gullible— it's another way the Church is trying to control you. You take that money you've been collecting for your parish and go get yourself a nice dress, fix yourself up, and go find some man or woman you can connect with—even for a moment. Because that's all that life is, Sister—a series of moments. Why don't you seize yours?

The NUN *nods at him and saunters off, obviously grappling with something. A passerby tries to stick money in her can, but she yanks it away.* LOKI *climbs over his seat and plops down beside the still-transfixed* BARTLEBY.

BARTLEBY (*looking* OC)

Here's what I don't get about you: you know for a fact that there is a God. You've been in His presence, He's talked to you personally. And yet I just heard you claim to be an atheist.

LOKI

I just like to fuck with the clergy, man—keep 'em on their toes.
(*looks around*)
Now here's what I don't get about you: why do you feel the need to come here all the time?

BARTLEBY (*off travelers*)

Because this is humanity at its best. Look at them.

A reunited FAMILY *share a group hug and move on, making way for two young* LOVERS *to embrace and kiss passionately.*

OC BARTLEBY

All that tension, all that anger and mistrust, forgotten for one perfect moment when they come off that plane. See those two? What the guy doesn't know is that the girl cheated on him while he was away.

OC LOKI

She did?

BARTLEBY *and* LOKI *continue to watch the arrivals.*

BARTLEBY

Twice. But it doesn't matter at this moment because they're both so relieved to be with one another. I like that. I just wish they could all feel that way more often.

LOKI

Is this why I had to miss my fucking cartoons this morning? You called, you said it was important, and I come all the way down here just to share in your half-assed obsessions with Hallmark moments?

BARTLEBY (*still looking* OC)

We're going home.

LOKI *freezes, mid-reach, and stares at his friend, shocked.* BARTLEBY *pulls an envelope from his jacket and extracts a newspaper article.*

BARTLEBY

Somebody sent us this in the mail.

He pushes the article and the popcorn toward LOKI, *who continues to stare at him.*

BARTLEBY

Take it, man. And quit leering at me. People are going to think I just broke up with you or something.

LOKI (*accepting article and corn*)

You *did* just say we're going home, didn't you?

BARTLEBY
Read.

LOKI (*off article*)
"Cardinal Glick Cuts Ribbon on 'Catholicism—Wow!'
Campaign." And?

BARTLEBY
You have to keep reading.

LOKI
"T.V. spots . . . papal consent . . . rededication . . . "
(*to Bartleby*)
Again—and?

BARTLEBY (*snatches article*)
Give me this.
(*reading*)
"The rededication of Saint Michael's Church . . .

INSERT T.V. NEWS FOOTAGE —

It's of Cardinal Glick's earlier Press Conference, and various shots of Saint Michael's Church. The Reporter's *voice-over gives way to an image of the Reporter himself, standing on the church steps.*

REPORTER
. . . is the kick-off of a new campaign that seeks to bring
Catholicism into the mainstream. With a papal sanction, the
archway entrance to the century-old, Jersey Shore house of
worship will serve as a passageway of plenary indulgence, a
little-known Catholic belief that offers all who pass through
its arches a morally clean slate. Thousands are expected to
turn out for the event this Friday, in what the new
movement's mastermind, Cardinal Ignatius Glick, has stated
" . . . is the biggest thing to happen to this little church since
the electric votive candles were installed." For *Sunday
Newsbrief*, I'm Grant Hicks.

INT AIRPORT—DAY

BARTLEBY *and* LOKI *walk toward a people-mover and step on.*

LOKI

I still don't get it.

BARTLEBY

If you walk through the church's front door on the day of the rededication ceremony, your soul is wiped clean of any and all existing sin, moreso than the sacrament of penance could ever offer. It's a plenary indulgence, man—rarely employed, but extremely legit. I don't know why I never thought of this before.

LOKI

So you're saying you and I can just walk through this doorway and go back home?

BARTLEBY

No—by passing through the doors, our sins are forgiven. Then all we have to do is die . . .

LOKI

Die?! I don't want to die.

BARTLEBY

You'd rather stay down here for a few more eons?

LOKI

No, but we don't even know if we *can* die. And what if we can, but this archway thing doesn't pan out? What then? Hell? Fuck that!

BARTLEBY

Impossible. If we cut off our wings and transubstantiate to complete human form, we become mortal. And if we die with clean souls, there's no way they can keep us out. We won't be angels anymore, but at least we get to go home.

LOKI (*beat*)

Who sent the paper?

BARTLEBY

Who cares who sent the paper? All that matters is that after all these years, we've found a loophole. He can't keep us out anymore. And once we're back in, I'm sure He'll just forgive and forget.

They pass the NUN, *who leans against a wall, still dazed.*

LOKI

Yeah, but this plenary indulgence thing is a church law, not
Divine Mandate. Church laws are fallible because they're
created by man.

BARTLEBY

One of the last sacred promises imparted to Peter the first
Pope by the Son of God before He left was "Whatever you
hold true on earth . . .

LOKI

. . . I'll hold true in Heaven."

BARTLEBY

It's dogmatic law. If the Pope says it's so, God must adhere;
this thing has a papal sanction . . .

LOKI (*beat; extends hand*)

Let it never be said that your anal retentive attention to detail
never yielded positive results.

BARTLEBY (*accepts hand*)

You can't be anal retentive if you don't have an anus.

LOKI

There's just one thing I think I should do before we leave—
something that might help get us back on His good side.

BARTLEBY

What's that?

LOKI *smiles and starts rifling through his pockets. He extracts a magazine
article.*

LOKI

This is something I've been dreaming about for five years
now. Read that.

*The crumpled article displays a gold-hued, cartoon cow, alongside various
profit charts and text.*

OC BARTLEBY

"Mooby the Golden Calf—Creating an Empire out of
Simplicity."

LOKI *nods to the article.*

LOKI

I want to hit them.

BARTLEBY

What're you, high?! We finally find a way back, and you
want to jeopardize it because you've got a soft spot for the
good ol' days?!

LOKI

What better way to show I've repented than by resuming the
position I once denied . . . thanks to you.

BARTLEBY

I really don't think a killing spree is going to make things
better for us!

LOKI

"Killing spree"? We're talking about Divine Justice here—
punishing the wicked, raining down fire and brimstone. He's
all about that. I *know* He'd want this done.

BARTLEBY

There hasn't been an Angel of Death since you quit. Doesn't
that mean anything to you? Besides, what if you're wrong?

LOKI

If I'm wrong—which I'm *not*—it won't matter. Like you
said—we pass through the arch and we're forgiven anyway.
No harm, no foul.

They step up to an elevator and press the button.

BARTLEBY (*considering it*)

Well . . . He *does* hate competition. And this Mooby deninitely
falls under that heading.

LOKI

The church we have to go to is where?

BARTLEBY

New Jersey. The rededication is in four days.

The doors open. They get on. Other people are inside as well.

> LOKI
> Our last four days on earth. If I had a dick, I'd go get laid. But
> we can do the next best thing.

> BARTLEBY
> What's that?

> LOKI
> Let's kill people.

A WOMAN *drinking coffee beside* LOKI *does a spit-take.* LOKI *smiles at her as the elevator doors close.*

> LOKI
> Oh, not you.

OPENING CREDITS

EXT SAINT STEPHEN'S PARISH—DAY

The church sits on a grassy knoll in McHenry—a suburb of Chicago. Some kids tear by on bikes and egg the announcements sign.

> OC PRIEST
> The greater Illinois chapter of the Right to Life foundation
> will be holding its biannual softball game against the Cook
> County Pro-Choice League next Sunday at two.

INT SAINT STEPHEN'S PARISH—DAY

The PRIEST *speaks from the lectern, addressing semi-filled rows of the faithful.*

> PRIEST
> Those who find the weekly demonstration outside of the
> Twelfth Street Planned Parenthood Clinic hard to make due
> to work schedules are urged to show their support in the
> fight against the thoughtless and wanton destruction of life
> by cheering on our boys on the field. Refreshments, as
> always, will be served.

Dollying down the rows while the Priest rattles on, we pass the parishio-ners. Some listen intently, others are nodding off. One surreptitiously lis-tens to a Walkman; a man and a woman quietly argue while their kid colors in a coloring book, going off the page and marking the pew; two kids play cards; one guy leafs through a copy of Hustler *hidden by his hymnal book.*

OC PRIEST

Today's second collection will be donated to the John Doe
Jersey Life Fund. For those of you who haven't been
following the news, an unidentified homeless man who was
accosted and severely beaten at the New Jersey shore last
Tuesday lies in critical but stable condition in one of that
area's hospitals. He lacks identification and police have had
no luck in tracking down any possible family. While he
shows no signs of recovery, the Arch-bishop of the Trenton
Diocese has disputed the state's decision to remove the
indigent man from life support systems, asking that Catholics
all over the country join in this protest against euthanasia.
And finally—will whoever keeps parking in my spot stop
doing that. Thank you. Now, please rise for the recession of
faith. We believe in one God, the father almighty . . .

As the congregation flatly joins in the prayer, we stop on BETHANY—*a beau-tiful thirty-something woman who struggles to stay awake. She checks her watch and exhales softly.*

GIRL V.O.

I don't really want to be here.

EXT PLANNED PARENTHOOD CLINIC—DAY

A small gaggle of sign-carrying Right-to-Lifers march in front of the building.

BETHANY V.O.

Fair enough. Pick a time or place you'd rather be.

INT BETHANY'S OFFICE—DAY

The source of the voice—a GIRL—*sits beside Bethany's desk, arms folded over her jacket.* BETHANY *leans back in her chair.*

GIRL
Are you, like, a shrink or something?

BETHANY
Would that I made what a shrink makes. But alas . . .
(thumbs her humble attire)
. . . Yo-ho, yo-ho, a counselor's life for me.

GIRL
I was on that ride.

BETHANY
Then it *is* a small world, after all. So come on—humor me:
any time, any place—where would you rather be right at this
moment?

GIRL
Back at the night my stupid boyfriend swore up and down he
was sterile.

BETHANY
And you believed him?

GIRL
I don't know. It made sense at the time. He has one of those
crooked dicks.

BETHANY *chuckles. The* GIRL *joins her. It's comfortable, finally. The first
part of Bethany's job complete, she moves on to phase two as she glances at
the girl's chart.*

BETHANY
Now this is your—what? Third time?

GIRL
The lecture begins. Actually, this might be the first time I really
listen. I mean, usually the counselor's some gross-looking lady.
You know how hard it is to listen to someone go on about
abortion when they're too ugly to get laid in the first place?

BETHANY
Alright—it's obvious you know the drill by now. And your
mind is made up about this, which is a plus. What say we
skip the lecture—as long as you promise to get on the pill and
use condoms in the future.

GIRL
If I take the pill, I gain weight.

BETHANY (*faux shock; reaches for phone*)
What?! I've never heard of such a thing! I've gotta call the AMA about this shocking new medical development!
(*hangs phone up*)
I used to feel the same way—I wouldn't go on the pill because it made me blow up. Take my word for it, though—it's worth the extra five pounds.

GIRL
Like you'd even notice it on you.

BETHANY (*filling out chart*)
You would if I were still on it.

GIRL
What do you use now?

BETHANY
I don't.

GIRL
You don't use anything? You? Why not?

BETHANY
That's a very personal and very boring story that I don't know you well enough to subject you to.

GIRL
You're religious, right? You don't use anything because you can't.

BETHANY
Yeah, I'm a real Bible-thumper. That's why I'm counseling you to use birth control as I go over the paperwork for your abortion.

GIRL
Then why don't you use birth control?

BETHANY
None of your beeswax.

                              GIRL
Oh, come on. I want to hear your sad tale of woe. Who
knows—maybe you'll tell me something so scary that I'll
never have to make this trip again.
                        BETHANY (*beat; sighs*)
Okay.
                        (*pulls out smokes*)
But feel free to nod out.
                        (*lights one*)
You know these girls that dated the same guy all through
high school?
                        (*the GIRL nods*)
Well, I was one of them. Brett Waits. We were in loooove.
Neither of us had a personal indentity because we were such
a hardcore couple. So much so that we decided to go to
Carnegie Mellon together . . . that's this college in Pittsburgh.
So there we are—away at school, and there's suddenly no
parents to worry about anymore. So we're screwing like
rabbits—just constantly doing it. And since I'm not on the pill
because the pill makes me gain weight, guess what
happened?

                              GIRL
You wound up getting pregnant.

                             BETHANY
And as if that wasn't harrowing enough—I tell my boyfriend,
and you know what he says?

                              GIRL
He tells you to get an abortion.

                             BETHANY
He begs me to have it.

                              GIRL
Get out of here.

                             BETHANY
Nope. He's suddenly filled with the desire to be a family
man. He's telling me we should quit school and get married.

I'm telling him that that'll screw up our educations. We
fought about it for a week—my argument being why rush to
have kids, you know? We could always have a baby in a
couple of years—after school. But he wouldn't hear of it. And
to make matters worse, he cornered me with an ultimatum—
either I was going to have this baby or we were breaking up.

GIRL

What a scumbag.

BETHANY

He's even got the Planned Parenthood all staked out—his
R.A.'s mother works there, so if I go in, I'm caught.

GIRL

Why didn't you just dump his ass?

BETHANY

We may have had different takes on the situation, but what
could I do? I was in love with him.
                                       (*beat*)
So, it's an old story, but . . . I started asking people about . . .
alternatives—to Planned Parenthood. And as it turned out, a
girl in my sorority had a cousin in med school—second year.

GIRL

Oh my God . . .

BETHANY

And before I know it, there's me—in nineteen eighty-one—on
the receiving end of what could be considered a cleaner and
slightly more advanced wire-hanger abortion. All because
I'm in love with my boyfriend.
                               (*beat; shakes it off*)
So it goes off without a hitch. I tell him I miscarried. He
nurses me for two weeks, because I was feeling really sick. I
figured it was the guilt. It takes all I have to keep from
breaking down and telling him the truth. But after awhile, the
lie becomes the truth. I'd miscarried. That was that. After
graduation, we got married and immediately set about trying
to have kids. We tried like hell for the first six months, but

nothing happened. So I went to my gynecologist to see if
everything was okay on my end.
>   (*smiles weakly*)
It wasn't.
>   (*beat*)
Seems that the instruments the med-school student was using
weren't as clean as they could have been. That sickness I felt
wasn't guilt—it was this infection, which over the course of
four or five years had left my uterus unable to sustain life. I'd
never be able to have a child.

The Girl's face says it all. BETHANY *takes a drag and continues.*

>   BETHANY
So there I am—devastated. And now I have to go home to
break the news to my husband who years before had begged
me to have the baby—his baby. But on top of that, I have to
tell him that I've been lying to him for five years, and that I'd
had that abortion he'd leveled his ultimatum against, and
because of it, we'd never have kids. Up to that moment in
life, I'd only taken drinks recreationally—parties, keggers,
bars. That was the first night I ever *needed* a drink—to give
me strength, oddly enough.
>   (*takes a drag*)
I unload on my husband through my tears; he just stares at
me through his. When I'm done, he sits on the couch and rubs
his eyes. And in the calmest, most rational voice I've ever
heard anybody use, he asks me for a divorce.

>   GIRL
No . . .

>   BETHANY
And I fought him, you know? I tried to talk him out of it; told
him there were alternatives—like we could adopt. And all he
said was he wanted a wife who could have *his* children.
>   (*beat*)
He remarried. He had two kids in two years with his new
wife. We never spoke again. And I started working for
Planned Parenthood.

The GIRL *is speechless.* BETHANY *manages a smile.*

> BETHANY
>
> Interesting postscript to that story—the med-school student?
> He dropped out two weeks after my abortion. Turns out he
> couldn't stand the sight of blood. He sells shoes in Monticello.
> *(smiles and puts out her smoke)*
> The five pounds'll go straight to your boobs—making you a
> god in your boyfriend's eyes. Trust me—take the five pounds.

INT A QUAINT SUBURBAN HOME—DAY

A doorbell ring is heard. A fortyish WOMAN *opens the door. Outside stands
an attractive (but pale) fellow named* AZRAEL. *He wears a hat.*

> AZRAEL
>
> Good afternoon, Mrs . . .
> *(looks at clipboard)*
> . . . Reynolds. I'm from the EPA. We're checking on possible
> freon leaks. Tell me—do you have air conditioning?

> WOMAN
>
> Yes—we have central air.

> AZRAEL
>
> In every room?

> WOMAN
>
> Except the bathroom. Why?

> AZRAEL *(to no one)*
>
> No central air in the bathroom? You do know what that
> means, don't you?

The WOMAN *jerks forward a bit, her outstretched arms clasping onto Azrael's
jacket as she collapses into him. He smiles at her.*

> AZRAEL
>
> Hot shit.

The WOMAN *drops to the ground, revealing a* STYGIAN TRIPLET *(the preteen
hockey youth from earlier). He holds a freshly bloodied hockey stick.* AZRAEL
steps over the Woman's body and past the TRIPLET, *heading toward the thermostat. He dials it to the lowest setting.*

AZRAEL

No pleasure, no rapture, no exquisite sin greater than central air. If we had something like this back home, maybe none of this would be necessary.

AZRAEL breathes in the cool air and sighs, as the TRIPLET *looks on. He nods to the Woman's body in the doorway.*

AZRAEL

Pick that up.

The STYGIAN TRIPLET *drags the Woman's body inside, as some kids ride past the house on bikes, oblivious to the horror. The door closes.*

INT QUAINT HOUSE LIVING ROOM—DAY

The TRIPLET *drags the body behind the couch. The other two* TRIPLETS *kneel on bended knee before* AZRAEL.

AZRAEL

This will be the base of operations from here on in. Now if I remember my protocol correctly, the powers will attempt to contact the Last Scion—which leaves us no other recourse than to eliminate her before she enters the fray. I need you three to shuffle her loose the mortal coil, so that we may obtain our final glory. Are we all on the same page?
        (*they nod*)
Good. Go.

The STYGIAN TRIPLETS *rise and exit.* AZRAEL *grabs a candy from a dish, chews it, and spits it out.*

AZRAEL

Who needs a bathroom, anyway?

EXT CLINIC—DAY

A well-dressed LIZ *maneuvers through the small throng of Right-to-Lifers. They shake their placards at her accusingly.*

PROTESTOR 1

You're gonna burn in hell, you fucking baby killer!

PROTESTOR 2

Tell her, Steve-Dave!

LIZ (*looking over their shoulders*)

Holy shit. It's the Pope.

As the throng turns excitedly, LIZ *ducks inside the clinic.*

INT CLINIC COFFEE ROOM—DAY

A newspaper headline fills the frame—"Church Says No to Death of John Doe." It's lowered to reveal BETHANY, *reading.* LIZ *enters and hangs up her coat.*

LIZ

Jesus! You're a Catholic, aren't you? Can't you talk to them or something?

BETHANY

They hate me more than you, no doubt. At least you have an excuse—you're Jewish. You don't know any better.

LIZ

I don't think they'd accept that one—we already used it as our excuse for killing Christ. So where were you yesterday morning? A bunch of us went out for brunch.

BETHANY

I went to church.

LIZ

That still kills me—you and church. If only they knew your weekly tithing came from a Planned Parenthood paycheck.

BETHANY

I don't know why I still go, Liz. I can remember going to church when I was young and being moved. Now I sit there and I feel nothing.

LIZ

So then why the weekly vigil?

BETHANY

You wouldn't believe me if I told you.

LIZ

You think I'm going to mock your religious beliefs? We're friends, Bethany—I may mock you for being a thirty-five-year old divorcée who's never had an orgasm, but I'd never mock you for having faith.

BETHANY

That's just it—I don't. I don't think I have any faith left.

LIZ (*making coffee*)

Remember that seminary student who used to mow my lawn? The one I tried to set you up with?

BETHANY

The twenty year old—the guy I could've baby-sat for in high school.

LIZ

Yeah, well the point is, one time, he told me something. He said that faith is like a glass of water. When you're young, the glass is small, and it's easy to fill up. But the older you get, the bigger the glass gets, and the same amount of liquid doesn't fill it anymore. Periodically, the glass has to be refilled.

BETHANY

You're suggesting I need to get filled?

LIZ (*collects her things to leave*)

In more ways than one. What are you doing tonight?

BETHANY

Watching t.v.

LIZ

You need to get laid, Bethany Sloane. You need a man. If only for ten minutes.

BETHANY

It's been my experience that the average male is never a man—not even for ten minutes in his entire life span.

LIZ

Uh-oh—that sounds militant. You thinking of joining the other side?

BETHANY
Couldn't do it. Women are insane.

LIZ
Then you'd better get back to church and ask God for a third option.

BETHANY
I think God is dead.

LIZ
The sign of a true Catholic.

LIZ exits with her coffee. BETHANY stares after her.

INT BETHANY'S BEDROOM—NIGHT

BETHANY in bed, sleeping. From the darkness, a creaking floorboard is heard. BETHANY reacts, grabbing a bat from under the bed. She peers into the darkness.

Suddenly, the room explodes in flames. A huge fire that appears to be shooting out from the floor ignites mere feet from Bethanyís bed. BETHANY leaps back, taking a beat to stare, mesmerized.

VOICE *(powerful; booming)*
BEHOLD THE METATRON—HERALD OF THE ALMIGHTY AND VOICE OF THE ONE TRUE GOD!

The VOICE repeats itself. BETHANY darts out of bed and dashes into her closet, quickly returning with a fire extinguisher. While the Voice is in mid-sentence, she blasts the flame with the contents of the canister, swirling the nozzle around to drench it. The booming Voice sputters and starts coughing, losing its impressive edge. BETHANY stops squirting and turns on her bedside lamp.

There stands a choking, drenched METATRON, coughing up some of the extinguisher's contents. He's doubled over, hacking. BETHANY stares, shocked.

METATRON
Sweet . . . Jesus! Did you . . . have to use . . . the whole can?!

BETHANY grabs her bat again and holds it up, this time offensively.

BETHANY

WHO THE FUCK ARE YOU AND WHAT THE FUCK ARE
YOU DOING IN MY ROOM?!

METATRON

I'm the one who's soaked and she's the one who's surly!
That's rich!

BETHANY (*reaching for phone, still holding bat*)
I'm calling the cops! Breaking and entering, attempted arson
. . . they're going to lock you up for life . . . !

METATRON (*wiping off clothes*)
No dial tone.

BETHANY (*ear to phone*)
You cut the phone lines . . .
              (*even more offensive with bat*)
Get the fuck out of here, now!

METATRON

Or you'll do what, exactly—hit me with that fish?

The bat BETHANY *held is now a salmon. She drops it to the floor and freaks.*

METATRON

Now just sit down on the bed and shut up!

BETHANY

Oh God—you're going to rape me . . .

METATRON

I'm not going to rape you.
              (*to himself; off clothes*)
Look at my suit . . . !

BETHANY

Take whatever you want, just don't kill or rape me . . .

METATRON

Enough with the raping already! I couldn't rape you if I
wanted to.
              (*unzips pants and pulls them down*)
Angels are ill-equipped.

BETHANY *stares. There, before her, stands the exposed* METATRON. *There is nothing where some sexual genitalia should be—it's as smooth and anatomically impaired as a Ken doll.*

> METATRON
> See? I'm as anatomically impaired as a Ken doll.
> (*pulls pants back up*)
> Make yourself useful and get me a towel.

BETHANY *grabs a nearby towel and tosses it to* METATRON, *who proceeds to towel himself off.*

> METATRON
> You bottom-feeders and your arrogance—you think everyone's just trying to get into your knickers.

> BETHANY
> Wh..what are you?

> METATRON
> I'm pissed off is what I am! You go around drenching everyone that comes into your room with flame-retardant chemicals? No wonder you're single.

METATRON *throws the towel back at the befuddled* BETHANY.

> METATRON
> Now—stand back.

METATRON *flexes and huge fucking wings extend from his back, dripping water.*

BETHANY *goes wide-eyed.*

> METATRON
> As I was saying, prior to your fire-fighting episode . . . I am the Metatron.

BETHANY *stares, saying nothing, pinned against the wall.* METATRON *looks insulted.*

> METATRON
> Don't tell me the name doesn't ring a bell?

BETHANY *remains silent and wide-eyed.* METATRON *gets testy.*

                          METATRON
You people. If there isn't a movie about it, it's not worth
knowing, is it?
                           (beat)
I am a seraphim.
                           (beat)
The highest choir of angels?
                           (beat)
You do know what an angel is, don't you?

BETHANY *slowly nods.*

                          METATRON
Metatron acts as the voice of God. Any documented occasion
when some yahoo claims God has spoken to them, they're
speaking to me. Or they're speaking to themselves.

                     BETHANY *(beat)*
Um . . . Why doesn't God speak for Himself?

                          METATRON
So glad you decided to join the conversation. To answer
that—human beings have neither the aural nor the
psychological capacity to withstand the awesome power of
God's true voice. Were you to hear it, your mind would cave
in and your heart would explode within your chest.
We went through five Adams before we figured that out.

                          BETHANY
Are you going to kill me?

                          METATRON
I could for what you did to this suit. Unfortunately I can't.
You're called.

                          BETHANY
Hunh?

                          METATRON
Millions of years since your ancestors dwelled in caves, and
your grasp of the language hasn't really risen above the
grunt. Color this angel impressed.

> BETHANY (*beat*)
> How do I know you're an angel?

> METATRON
> Oh, you mean aside from the fiery entrance and the expansive wingspan? You want more proof? Fine. How about a tequila?
> (*snaps fingers*)

INT MEXICAN BAR—NIGHT

BETHANY *and* METATRON *sit at a table.* BETHANY *immediately clutches at her pajamas.* METATRON *waves a* WAITER *over.*

> BETHANY
> Where the hell are we?!

> METATRON
> The only place you can go for good tequila.
> (*to* WAITER)
> Dos tequilas, por favor. And an empty glass.

> WAITER
> Sí.

> (*he exits*)

> METATRON
> Gracias, senor.

> BETHANY
> We're in Mexico?!

> METATRON
> Actually, we're in the franchised Mexican family eatery down the street from your apartment. But it's impressive nonetheless. You don't mind that I lost the wings, do you? I'm trying to keep our profile low.

> BETHANY
> I suppose it would be too cliché to observe aloud that this is the weirdest dream I've ever had.

> METATRON
> Can you imagine how insulting it is to converse with a person and have them insist you're a dream? If I had an ego, it'd be bruised.

BETHANY
What do you want with me?

METATRON
I'm to charge you with a holy crusade.
(*pause*)
You do know what a crusade is, don't you?

BETHANY *offers him a "What are you—an asshole or something?" look.*

METATRON
Don't give me that. Last time I charged someone with a
crusade they had to look the word up.

BETHANY
Why am I supposed to go on a crusade?

METATRON
Yours is a heritage divine. Also, you didn't seem to be doing
too much lately.

The WAITER *arrives with their drinks.*

METATRON
Oh—Gracias!
(WAITER *leaves; off the tequila*)
One of the only things your kind has mastered since you
crawled from the primordial ooze.

BETHANY
I work in an abortion clinic.

METATRON (*spits tequila into empty glass*)
Noah was a drunk. Look what he accomplished. And no
one's even asking you to build an ark. All you have to do is
go to New Jersey.

BETHANY
New Jersey.

METATRON
Sure. Go to New Jersey and visit a small church on a very
important day. Agreed?

BETHANY

That doesn't sound like much of a crusade.

METATRON

Aside from the fine print, that's it.

BETHANY

And what's the fine print?

METATRON (*mumbles into glass*)

stopacoupleofangelsfromenteringandthusnegatingallexistence.

BETHANY

Wait, wait, wait. Repeat that.

METATRON (*spits into empty glass*)

Stop a couple of angels from entering and thus negating all existence. I hate when people need it spelled out for them.

BETHANY

You might want to clarify that.

METATRON

That's the problem with you people—you need everything clarified. No leaps of faith whatsoever. Alright—you want the whole secret origin? Here goes: Back in the old days, God was vengeful and hot-tempered, and His wrath was bore by the Angel of Death—name of Loki. When Sodom and Gomorrah were destroyed? That was Loki. When the waters wiped out everything with the exception of Noah and his menagerie? That was Loki. And he was good at what he did. But one day, he refused to bear God's wrath any longer.

BETHANY

Why?

METATRON

Because he listened to his friend—a Grigori by the name of Bartleby.

BETHANY

Grigori?

METATRON

One of the choirs of angels. They're called Watchers. Guess what they do?

(*beat*)

So one day, Loki's wiping out all the firstborn of Egypt . . .

BETHANY

The Tenth Plague.

METATRON

See? Tell a person you're the Metatron and they stare at you blankly; mention something out of a Charlton Heston movie and they're suddenly theology scholars. May I continue uninterrupted?

(BETHANY *nods*)

So once he's done with the firstborn, Loki takes his friend Bartleby out for a post-slaughter drink. And over many rounds, they get into this discussion about whether or not murder in the name of God is okay. Now, Bartleby can run circles around Loki intellectually, not to mention the fact that Loki's more than half in the bag, and in the end, Bartleby convinces Loki to quit his position and take a lesser one—one that doesn't involve slaughter. So—very inebriated—Loki tells God he quits; throws down his fiery sword, gives Him the finger—which ruins it for the rest of us, because from that day forward, God decreed that angels could no longer imbibe alcohol. Hence all the spitting.

BETHANY

Sounds reasonable.

METATRON

Maybe to you, but I'm a lush by nature.

BETHANY

I mean about the Angel of Death's resignation.

METATRON

For a liberal, yes, but this is the Angel of Death we're talking about. The Angel of Death can't be a conscientious objector. The Angel of Death is charged with meting out whatever justice God demands. So for their insolence, God decreed that neither Loki nor Bartleby would ever be allowed back into Paradise.

BETHANY

Were they sent to Hell?

METATRON

Worse. Wisconsin. For the entire span of human history. And
when the world ends, they'll have to sit outside the gates for
all eternity.

BETHANY

And this has what to do with me?

METATRON

Somebody's clued them in to a loophole in Catholic dogma
that would allow them to reenter Heaven.

BETHANY

So what? They beat the system. Good for them.

METATRON

It's not that simple. If they get in, they will have reversed
God's decree. Now listen closely, because this part is very
important. Existence in all its form and splendor functions
solely on one principle: God is infallible. To prove God wrong
would undo reality and everything that is. Up would become
down, black would become white, existence would become
nothingness. In essence—if they are allowed to enter that
church, they'll unmake the world.

BETHANY

Are these guys that bitter?

METATRON

No. They have no idea what their actions will result in. As far
as they know, they're just going home.

BETHANY

If this is so major, why are you talking to me? Why doesn't
God do something about it?

METATRON

He could. He could blink them out of existence, destroy that
church, turn them into plants. But He'd rather see you take
care of this one personally.

BETHANY

Why me?

METATRON

Because of who you are.

BETHANY

And who am I?

METATRON

The girl in the p.j.'s. Don't ask so many questions—just serve your purpose.

BETHANY

I'll pass.

METATRON

I beg your pardon?

BETHANY

When some quiet little infection destroyed my uterus—where was God? When my husband decided he couldn't be with a wife that couldn't bear his children—where was God? Now after all these years of noninvolvement in my life, He sends one of His lackeys my way who tells me I should save the world, and as what—some sort of test? To Hell with Him.

METATRON

Do yourself a favor, Bethany—do the world a favor: let go of your petty crap. It's served you precious little in the past, and it serves you even less now when the fate of existence hangs in the balance. Don't allow eons of history and life to get blinked out of being just because you have a grudge against your creator.

BETHANY

A grudge?

METATRON

And any other day I'd say that's your business and your life, and enjoy yourself and goodnight. But this isn't about you—this is about everybody. So you lost the ability to make life. You're being offered the chance to play mother to the world by acting like one and protecting it—saving it.

(swigs Bethany's drink and spits it out)
But I can't make you. However, should you decide to stop
being selfish and accept your responsibility, you won't be
alone. You'll have support.

BETHANY

Let me guess—more angels?

METATRON

Prophets—in a manner of speaking. Two of them. The one
who speaks—and he will at great lengths, whether you want
him to or not—will make mention of himself as a prophet.
The other one . . . well, he's the quiet type.
(looks at watch)
I have to go. You'll do what you will. But try to remember—
we're working in a time frame here.

METATRON *heads off.*

BETHANY

Hey.

METATRON *turns back toward* BETHANY.

BETHANY

You work for God?

METATRON

They tell me it's God. If it's not, I'm going to be severely
pissed—what with all these years of expectorating perfectly
good tequila.

BETHANY

What's He like?

METATRON

God?
(thinks)
Lonely. But funny. He's got a great sense of humor. Take sex,
for example—there's nothing funnier than the ridiculous
faces you people make, mid-coitus.

BETHANY

Sex is a joke in Heaven?

> METATRON
> The way I understand it, it's mostly a joke down here too.

METATRON *produces maracas from nowhere. He shakes them at* BETHANY.

> METATRON
> I'll see you.

He tosses them at her. BETHANY *catches them, and we pull back to reveal she is surrounded by a mariachi band, seranading her.*

INT BETHANY'S BEDROOM—NIGHT

BETHANY *is startled awake by her clock radio. She moves to lie back down, but feels something. She pulls out the set of maracas from under her pillow.*

INT BETHANY'S OFFICE—DAY

BETHANY *sits at her desk, staring into space. A twenty-something girl speaks, but* BETHANY *is not really listening. She's extremely preoccupied.*

INT CLINIC—NIGHT

BETHANY *shuts off the lights in the various rooms. She packs up her bag and turns on the alarm.*

EXT CLINIC—NIGHT

BETHANY *exits and locks the door behind her. She starts walking.*

As her feet tread lightly toward her car, three small shadows move toward her.

BETHANY *throws her bag on her car roof and rummages through her purse for her keys. She hears something and stops. Rollerblades can be heard moving slowly across the asphalt of the parking lot.* BETHANY *turns quickly.*

Nobody's there. She looks around, a bit perturbed, keys in hand.

> BETHANY (*calling into the darkness*)
> God, what time do you people quit and go home?! Let's just save it for tomorrow, alright?

There's no response. Then there's the noise of wood being tapped against the ground. BETHANY *peers into the darkness, looking for the source.*

BETHANY *jams her keys into the door, frantically trying to get into the car. Suddenly, she's checked into the car.* BETHANY *goes down, her keys landing slightly in front of her. She scrambles toward the keys, as a blade crashes down on them. She looks up to see a* STYGIAN TRIPLET *standing before her. He smacks her keys past her, and they slide under the car.* BETHANY *looks up again to see the other two* TRIPLETS *now. They tap their hockey sticks in unison on the ground. They emit an unholy shriek and charge her.* BETHANY *turns away from them, flailing around under the car for her keys, which are just out of reach.*

Suddenly, two figures swoop down from above, landing on the ground between BETHANY *and her menacers.*

SMALLER FIGURE
SNOOTCH TO THE MOTHERFUCKING NOOOOOOTCH!!!

In a series of quick cuts, we see glimpses of a fight, while the oblivious BETHANY *scrambles to reach her keys under the car. Open palms strike pre-teen faces, slashing sticks are ducked, jerseys are pulled over heads, skaters are clotheslined and checked.*

BETHANY *finally reaches her keys and spins around, only to see . . .*

The STYGIAN TRIPLETS *skating off rapidly into the distance. Two figures enter into Bethany's line of sight, their backs to her. Then, we get a shimmery look at the heroes, reflected in a puddle on the ground.*

SMALLER FIGURE
GO BACK TO YOUR PAPER ROUTES, YOU PUNK FUCKS!

We pan up off the puddle to reveal JAY *and* SILENT BOB.

JAY
Snoogans.

They turn to BETHANY. JAY *is all excited;* SILENT BOB *helps* BETHANY *to her feet.*

JAY
Did you see that shit?! I know they were just kids, but we kicked their fucking pube-less asses!

BETHANY

I don't know what to say . . . or think . . . except . . .

JAY

That you wanna offer us sex as a reward.

BETHANY

Um . . . that I'd like to know who they and you are.

JAY

Oh. I'm Jay, and this is my hetero lifemate, Silent Bob. I don't know who those kids were, but they would've kicked yours and Lunchbox's ass if I hadn't represented.

BETHANY

Well . . . thank you for being out here so late . . .
                              (*freezes*)
Wait a second—are you protestors?

JAY

What's a protestor?

BETHANY

You're not with the Right-to-Lifers?

JAY

You mean those dickheads with the signs and pictures of dead babies? Shit no! Me and Silent Bob are pro-choice: a woman's body is her own fucking business.

BETHANY

Then—I don't mean to sound ungrateful—but what are you doing hanging around?

JAY

We're here to pick up chicks.

BETHANY (*a bit stunned*)

Excuse me?

JAY

We figure an abortion clinic is a good place to meet loose women. Why else would they be there unless they like to fuck?

BETHANY (*taken aback*)

Oh. Right. Well, I should be going. Thanks for the rescue . . . I think.

JAY (*shocked*)
Wait, wait, wait—we just saved your ass, and you're just
going to take off? What the shit is that?

BETHANY
I had a weird night last night, and tonight's not shaping up to
be any better. I think I should go home, take some Percocets,
and lie down.
(*opens her car door*)
JAY (*to Silent Bob*)
Now how about that shit? Fuck this town, man—I'm going
back to Jersey and starting up the business again.
(*they start walking*)
I can kick the shit out of little kids in Red Bank while trying to
make myself a profit.

BETHANY *freezes. Metatron's words echo in her ear. She shakes her head.*

BETHANY (*to herself*)
You've gotta be kidding me.
(*thinks for a beat; then*)
Hey! Wait!

She runs up to them. They whip around and raise their fists defensively.

BETHANY
Sorry.
(*beat*)
Would you . . . I can't believe I'm doing this . . .
(*inhales deeply*)
Would you . . . like to have a drink with me?

Jay's face lights up. He punches SILENT BOB *in the arm.*

JAY
See?! I told you if we hung around outside that place we'd
get laid! Thank you!
(*looking skyward*)
Thank you, God!

INT GUN SHOP—NIGHT

Various guns are laid out atop a glass case.

> OC SALESMAN
>
> Now this piece we call the "Fecal-ator"—one look at it, and the target shits him or herself. Try it on.

LOKI *picks up the gun.* BARTLEBY *and the* SALESMAN *look at him.*

> LOKI
>
> It's a lot more compact than the flaming sword, but not nearly as impressive. It doesn't have that "wrath-of-the-Almighty" edge to it. How am I supposed to strike fear into the hearts of the wicked with this thing? Look at this.

> SALESMAN
>
> Oh, I get it. You want to become a vigilante, right? Like Batman or something.

> LOKI
>
> Batman never uses guns.
> *(off gun)*
> I don't know. It feels impersonal.

> BARTLEBY
>
> Then don't use a gun. Lay the place to waste like.

> LOKI
>
> Easy for you to say—you get off light in a razing. You got to stand there and read at Sodom and Gomorrah. I had to do all the work.

> BARTLEBY
>
> What work? You lit a few fires.

> LOKI
>
> I rained down sulfur, man. There's a subtle difference.

> BARTLEBY
>
> I'm sure.

> LOKI
>
> Fuck you—any moron with a pack of matches can start a fire. Raining down sulfur is like an endurance trial. Mass genocide

is the most exhausting activity one can engage in, next to soccer.

> (*to* SALESMAN)
> I'll take this one.

SALESMAN
Five seventy-five and you can walk with it right now.

LOKI *drops a wad of bills on the counter and toys with his new gun.*

BARTLEBY
Soccer?

INT DINER—NIGHT

An English muffin is covered with a knifeful of jam. BETHANY *raises the bread to her mouth and takes a bite. She glances at the* OC *pair and stops chewing.*

JAY *and* SILENT BOB *study her intently.* JAY *smiles widely, anticipatory, and nods.*

All three sit at a small table near a window. BETHANY *puts the English muffin down and brushes off her hands. Jay's feet are moving a mile a minute.*

BETHANY
Are you both from around here?

JAY
Do you have a friend for Silent Bob, or are you going to do us both? If so, I'm first. I hate sloppy seconds.

BETHANY
You're a man of principle. Where do you come from?

JAY
This town in Jersey where we know, like, *everybody*.

BETHANY
Jersey's pretty far from McHenry——may I ask what brought you here?

JAY
Some fuck named John Hughes.

BETHANY (*thinks and catches on*)
Sixteen Candles John Hughes?

JAY
So you know the guy too? That fucking guy . . .
(*shakes his head*)
Made this flick called *Sixteen Candles*. Not bad—there's tits in
it, but no bush. But Ebert over here don't give a shit about
that, 'cuz he's, like, in love with this John Hughes guy. Goes
out and rents all his movies: fucking *Breakfast Club*, about
these stupid kids that actually *show up* for detention; fucking
Weird Science, where this broad wants to take her gear off and
get down, but oh, no, she don't because it's a PG movie; and
Pretty in Pink, which I can't watch with tubby over here
anymore, 'cuz every time it gets to the part where the red-
head hooks up with her dream guy, he starts sobbing like a
little girl with a skinned knee and shit. And there's nothing
worse than watching a fucking fat man weep . . .

BETHANY (*speeding him along*)
So what *exactly* brought you to Illinois?

JAY
Oh yeah. See, all these movies take place in a town called
Shermer, in Illinois—where all the honeys are top-shelf, but
all the dudes are whiny pussies. Except Judd Nelson—he was
harsh. But best of all, there was no one *dealing*, man. Then it
hits me—we could live like phat-rats if we were the blunt-
connection in Shermer, Illinois. So we collected some money
we were owed, and caught a bus. But you know what the
fuck we found out when we got there? There *is* no Shermer in
Illinois. Fucking movies are bullshit.

BETHANY
And now you live here?

JAY
Shit no. This burg sucks. It's too cold, and everyone's got a
stupid accent so you don't know what the fuck they're
saying.

BETHANY

When are you leaving?

JAY

When you're ready to skip out and make with the love.

BETHANY

No—I mean, when are you going back to New Jersey?

JAY (*to* SILENT BOB)

Jesus—this broad asks a lot of questions.

(*to* BETHANY)

Tomorrow.

BETHANY (*thinks*)

Tomorrow . . .

JAY

Yeah. So do you do anal? Is it true that chicks fart if you blast them in the ass?

BETHANY

I didn't ask you out for sex.

JAY

I'll take head.

BETHANY

This is going to sound really bad . . . I can't believe I'm even thinking about this, but . . .

(*composes herself*)

. . . I think I should go with you.

JAY

What, like steady? You wanna be my girlfriend?

(*shrugs to* SILENT BOB)

Alright, but Silent Bob has to live with us and you pay the rent.

BETHANY

No, I want to go with you to New Jersey.

JAY

Really? You're the only chick I ever met that wanted to go *to* Jersey. Most chicks try to get out.

BETHANY
When can we leave?

JAY
Wait a second—you want to go to New Jersey right now?
What about the sex? Are we going to fuck or not?

BETHANY
You're going to lead me somewhere.

JAY
Me lead *you*? Lady, look at me—I don't even know where *I*
am half the time. If we're not gonna fuck, then what the fuck
did you ask us out for?

BETHANY
Someone told me I'd meet you, and you'd take me
somewhere I was supposed to go.

JAY
What the hell are you babbling about? All I know is we saved
your ass from some angry fucking dwarves and you
promised us sex . . .
                    (*to* SILENT BOB)
Didn't this crazy broad promise us sex?
                    (*to* BETHANY)
. . . and now you're telling me that I'm supposed to take you
somewhere, and you don't even know where it is?!

BETHANY
                    (*beat*)
Do you believe in God?

JAY (*horrified*)
Holy fuck—all the fine, immoral bitches coming out of that
place, and we gotta get the one Jesus freak!
                    (*to* SILENT BOB, *getting up*)
Let's get the fuck outta here . . .
            BETHANY (*grabbing his sleeve*)
No, wait . . .

JAY (*pulling back*)
I'll scream rape.

BETHANY
I can pay you.

JAY (*quickly sitting back down*)
Pay?

BETHANY
A hundred bucks for being my guide. You were going to
Jersey anyway; all I'm asking is to tag along.

JAY (*thinks; to* SILENT BOB)
I feel like I'm Han Solo, you're Chewie, and she's Ben Kenobi,
and we're in that fucked-up bar!
(*to* BETHANY)
What about sex?

BETHANY
No sex.

JAY
Alright, but let's say we're caught in a situation where we've
got like five minutes to live, like a bomb or something is
gonna go off—would you fuck us then?

BETHANY
In that highly unlikely situation?
(*beat*)
Yeah, sure.

JAY
Yeah?
(*to* SILENT BOB)
She's a slut. Bunnnnng!
(*beat*)
I don't know—what do you think?

SILENT BOB *shrugs.* JAY *stands up.*

JAY
Alright. But I get to drive.

EXT MAIN HIGHWAY—NIGHT

Bethany's car roars past, speeding down the road, revving awfully loudly.

INT BETHANY'S CAR—NIGHT

The speedometer reads ninety-five.

JAY drives, eyes glued to the road, happy as hell. SILENT BOB *smokes.* BETHANY *sits pinned against the back seat. She struggles to lean forward. The engine still races.*

> BETHANY
> What gear are you in?!

> JAY
> Gear?

INT BETHANY'S ENGINE—NIGHT

The hood opens, and through the billowing smoke we see JAY, BOB, *and* BETHANY.

> JAY *(defensively)*
> Well, what do I know from shifting?! Like I ever drove before!

EXT HIGHWAY—NIGHT

BETHANY *walks away from the smoking car, shaking her head.* SILENT BOB *begins tinkering around with the engine as a cross-country bus races by.*

INT BUS—NIGHT

BARTLEBY *and* LOKI *sit in the back.* BARTLEBY *reads a map and* LOKI *tries to nap. A* COUPLE *makes out in the seat in front of them.*

> BARTLEBY
> Indiana, Ohio, Pennsylvania, then New Jersey.

> LOKI
> Don't forget Pittsburgh.

> BARTLEBY
> Oh right. The Angel of Death Returns. Sounds like a bad movie.

LOKI

Keep it up—the last time you started giving me shit about my
job, we got sentenced to life in Wisconsin.

(*lays head back*)

Besides . . . movies are bullshit.

BARTLEBY

(*looks out window for a beat*)

Didja ever wonder why—all this time we've been down
here—we never had the balls to leave the Cheese?

LOKI

I remember why—He said to stay where He put us. We were
all piss-scared He'd send us someplace worse than Wisconsin
if we disobeyed Him again.

BARTLEBY

Right.

(*beat*)

Where *were* we afraid He'd send us?

LOKI

New Jersey.

BARTLEBY *shakes his head, then looks out the window.* LOKI *tries to nap.*
Then . . .

BARTLEBY

You know, maybe you're wrong about this slaughter thing.
How can you even be sure of what incurs the Lord's wrath
these days? Times change. I remember when eating meat on
Friday was supposed to be a Hell-worthy trespass.

LOKI

The major sins never change. And besides—I can spot a
commandment breaker a mile away. Bet on it.

BARTLEBY

This coming from the guy who still owes me ten bucks from
that bet over which was going to be the bigger movie—*E.T.* or
Krush Groove.

LOKI (*bolts upright, pissed*)
Fuck you, man—time's gonna tell on that one! Are you
insinuating I don't have what it takes anymore?

BARTLEBY
Insinuating? No—I'm flat-out telling you.

LOKI *is seething. He looks around. His eyes fall on the make-out couple.*

LOKI
There. There's one.

BARTLEBY (*off couple*)
So? They're kissing.

LOKI
Adultery.

BARTLEBY
How do you know they're not dating?

LOKI
You'd know better than I would—am I right or what?

BARTLEBY
Oh, I know the truth, but I want to see how boned up on the
job you are: what's your proof?

LOKI
He's wearing a wedding band.

BARTLEBY
Has it occurred to you that maybe *she's* his wife?

LOKI
No married man kisses his wife like that.

BARTLEBY
You know—all I'm saying is it's a good thing you were never
the deciding member on a jury or anything.
(*looks back out window; as* LOKI)
"No married man kisses his wife like that."

BARTLEBY *goes back to staring out the window.* LOKI *then opens his eye.*
He thinks for a beat, then leans forward to the couple in front of him. He
nudges the MAN.

                                          LOKI

Excuse me.

The Couple stops kissing. The MAN *looks at* LOKI.

                                          LOKI

Are you married?

                                          MAN

Why?!

                                          LOKI

Just curious.

                              MAN (*holds up ringed ring-finger*)

What do you think?

The MAN *shakes his head and goes back to kissing.* BARTLEBY *offers* LOKI *a*
"Satisfied?" expression. LOKI *taps the* MAN *on the shoulder. The* MAN *turns*
again, pissed.

                                          MAN

What?!

                                          LOKI

To her?

                                          MAN

What?

                                          LOKI

Are you married to her?

                                          MAN

Not that it's any of your fucking business, but no! Why?!

LOKI *makes* BARTLEBY's *face back at him, calmly pulls the gun from his coat,*
and points it at the Man's head.

EXT HIGHWAY—NIGHT

A gunshot rings out. Screaming ensues as the bus skids to a halt. People
flock off in panic, scattering. After a beat, BARTLEBY *and* LOKI *deboard and*
stand there alone.

                              LOKI (*beat; singing as he walks away*)

"Whose house? . . . Run's house! . . . Whose house? . . . "

EXT ROADSIDE OF HIGHWAY—DAWN

SILENT BOB *and* JAY *still tinkering under the hood.* BETHANY *steams off to the side.*

> JAY (*to* SILENT BOB)
> She's fucking pissed, dude. She'll never fuck us now. Well, maybe you, but definitely not me.
> (*beat*)
> Let me know how she is.

> BETHANY (*turns on him*)
> Nobody is fucking me! You got that?! I don't know what I was thinking in that diner, but being that I've decided to go home and *not* to New Jersey, this is where I say good luck with finding Molly Ringwald or whoever you're looking for, sorry for the inconvenience, and "goodbye."

BETHANY *starts walking away.* JAY *stares at her, shocked. He chases after her.*

> JAY
> You're breaking up with us? Who the hell do you think you are, lady? You can't go around breaking people's hearts like that! I fell in love with you! *We* fell in love with you! Guys like us don't just fall out of the sky, you know!

On cue, a naked black MAN *falls from the sky, landing between the two parties.* BETHANY *and* JAY *stare at him.* BETHANY *drops to her knees and rolls him over, feeling for a pulse.* JAY *looks down, then looks skyward as* SILENT BOB *joins him.*

> JAY (*yelling up*)
> Beautiful, naked women don't just fall out of the sky, you know?!
> (*beat; to* SILENT BOB)
> Was worth a try.

SILENT BOB *nods.* BETHANY *presses her ear to the man's chest.*

> BETHANY
> No heartbeat.

JAY

Do you think someone threw him out of a plane with a message
written on him—like in *Con Air*? Did you see that flick?

MAN

Oh yeah—did *that* suck!

BETHANY, JAY, *and* SILENT BOB *leap back. The* MAN *sits up and rubs his face.*

JAY

KILL IT!! KILL IT!!

MAN

That sounds familiar.

BETHANY

Jesus, are you okay?

MAN

It's Rufus. And yeah, I'm fine.

JAY

He's the fuckin' undead!! Cut his head off!!

RUFUS (*getting up with Bethanyís help*)

What happened to your car? You clock ninety in first gear or
something?

JAY

Mind your own fucking business!

RUFUS (*to* JAY)

Hey—what I just did was not easy and it gave me a fucking
migraine. So if you don't pipe down, I'm going to yank your
sack off like a paper towel.

JAY (*hiding behind* SILENT BOB)

I knew it! Motherfucker wants to eat my brain!

BETHANY

I think he was aiming a bit further south.

(*to* RUFUS)

Speaking of which, you're awfully nude—Rufus, is it?

RUFUS

Rufus it is, miss. It's usually "Long Rufus," but it's a little
cold out here, you understand.

(*to* SILENT BOB)
Hey, tubby . . . how's about lending a brother your coat 'til I
can find my own threads?

JAY *looks at* SILENT BOB.

JAY
Dude, he fell out of thin air!

SILENT BOB *shrugs and passes his coat to* RUFUS. JAY *bugs.*

JAY
Dude, his piece is gonna be rubbing all over the inside of
your armor!

RUFUS
I'll do my best to tuck it back, brother.

SILENT BOB *nods as* RUFUS *pulls on the coat.*

BETHANY
You know, it's been years since I took physics, but I'd say that
fall should have liquefied you.

RUFUS
Death is a worry of the living. The dead—like myself—only
worry about decay and necrophiliacs.

JAY
See! I told you he was the undead!

RUFUS
Not the undead, the dead. I died. Christ told me the secret to
resurrection once when we were at a wedding in Cana, but I
got drunk and forgot it.

BETHANY (*incredulous*)
Wait, wait, wait—Christ? You knew Christ?

RUFUS
Knew him? I saw him naked.

BETHANY
Let me guess—you're another angel?

RUFUS
No, I'm a man—just like you and him.

(*looks at* JAY)

Well, maybe not like him. At least I *was* a man. Been dead
nearly two thousand years. Here.

(*pulls rolled-up paper from behind his ear*)

JAY

No wonder he saw Jesus—homey's rockin' the ganj.

BETHANY

It's not a joint.

(*unrolls it and studies*)

I can't read this.

RUFUS

It's Aramaic. It says "Rufus—see you in two years. Jesus."
Freaked me out because he basically told me when my
number was up. Took the flavor out of the remaining years.
Look, we gotta keep moving or those things'll get a bead on
you again. What say we continue this discussion over
something to eat? I'm starving.

He heads away, passing JAY, *who strikes a defensive pose.*

RUFUS

Back off, Kato.

BETHANY (*snaps*)

WAIT A SECOND!

(*inhales deeply*)

Between guys with wings, guys falling out of the sky, and
guys trying like mad to fuck me, I'd like to think I've been a
good sport about all this so far. But I'm not going anywhere
until I find out where the hell you came from?!

RUFUS

Me? I came from Heaven.

(*walking away*)

Let's start walking.

JAY

Walk? Fuck you! Do you know how far we are from
anywhere?

RUFUS

Back in the old days with J.C., we used to walk everywhere.
Did you ever hear of a fat apostle?

He exits. BETHANY *looks to* JAY *and* SILENT BOB *for some guidance or stability.*

JAY

What the hell's an apostle?

BETHANY *shakes her head and exits.* JAY *and* SILENT BOB *shrug at each other.*

EXT MOOBY CORP. BUILDING—DAWN

A large office building in downtown Pittsburgh, emblazoned with the corporate logo of the Mooby Corporation. A pickup truck pulls curbside in front of the structure, and BARTLEBY *and* LOKI *jump out of the back, offering waved thank-yous to the driver as he pulls away.* LOKI *pulls an onion out of his coat and tosses it in the air playfully. He nods to* BARTLEBY, *smiling as the pair head toward the entrance of the building.*

INT QUAINT SUBURBAN HOUSE—DAWN

The bruised and worn STYGIAN TRIPLETS *are seated on a couch. They look scared.* AZRAEL *paces in front of them.*

AZRAEL

Let me get this straight—she's already met the Prophets, and the Apostle's with them?

The STYGIAN TRIPLETS *nod.*

AZRAEL

Which means she grows closer to learning her true identity—
if she hasn't already. This . . . is . . . distressing . . .
(*beat*)
Well, I can't afford to go into the field—that'd only
compromise us further. It would seem that the best course of
action at this point is to insure that our parcel is not found.
And being that I can't even trust you enough to kill a woman,
I'm left with no choice but to seek outside assistance in
guarding said package.

(*sighs*)
I'm going to have to summon the Golgothan.

AZRAEL *exits. The* STYGIAN TRIPLETS *register shock. After a beat,* AZRAEL *comes back in.*

AZRAEL
Wait—why am *I* leaving? You guys get out of here—this is my office. Go put some peroxide on those cuts.

EXT FAST FOOD JOINT—DAWN

RUFUS—*now wearing some funky new clothes—carries a tray of fast food to an outdoor table. Sitting already are* BETHANY, JAY, *and* SILENT BOB. *A car full of* TEENS *heads toward them.*

RUFUS (*off new clothes*)
Dinner and new threads—one-stop shopping.

TEEN IN CAR (*yelling from passenger side*)
GARBAGE PICKER!

RUFUS (*waves to them*)
Thank you, ladies! Yes!
(*to group*)
What's that mean—"garbage picker"? Is it new slang—like calling a brother "fly"?

JAY
It means they saw you pull your outfit out of that Dumpster. They're mocking you, yo.

RUFUS (*yelling off at long-gone car*)
KISS MY DEAD, BLACK ASS!
(*handing coat back to* SILENT BOB)
I appreciate the loan, brother. You can have this back.

JAY (*to* SILENT BOB)
Lucky you.

RUFUS
Damn, I remember when all we used to have for breakfast was fish and goat's milk. What do you call this shit?

BETHANY (*to* RUFUS)

Egga Mooby Muffin. Now how about you start explaining
some things to me. Like—for starters—who the hell were
those kids that attacked me outside of the clinic?

RUFUS

Nasty little bastards called the Stygian Triplets. Just your
average neighborhood bored teens who—when they were
alive—snatched a neighbor's toddler and smashed its skull
in. "Just to see what it looked like," I believe was the reason
they gave. They were killed in a car wreck on the way to a
detention center.

BETHANY

So they're dead too?

RUFUS

You'd be surprised how many dead people are just walking
around—we're stubborn bastards. Thing is, those kids are
supposed to be in Hell. Which means that someone wants
you out of the picture so badly they're willing to summon
demons.

BETHANY

Is it those two angels I'm supposed to stop?

RUFUS

Couldn't be. They're not evil—they're just stupid.

JAY (*to* BETHANY)

Are you going to listen to this shit? We don't even know who
this guy is. For all you know, he's in with those fucks. They
both showed up at the same time.

BETHANY

I hate to say it—but he does have a point. How did you know
where to find us?

RUFUS

You know what the dead do with most of their time? Watch
the living. Especially in the shower.

JAY (*to* SILENT BOB)

I can't wait to die.

BETHANY

And why are you watching me?

RUFUS

Because you're the one who's going to help me get some
changes made in that book you all put so much stock in.

JAY

Hustler?

RUFUS

The Bible.

BETHANY

What's your beef with the Bible?

RUFUS

For starters? I'm not in it.

JAY

Neither are any of us, but you don't hear us bitching and
moaning.

RUFUS

But I'm supposed to be in it. I was the Thirteenth Apostle.

BETHANY, JAY, *and* SILENT BOB *laugh.*

BETHANY

I've been going to church my entire life and I've never heard
of a thirteenth apostle named Rufus.

RUFUS

See? You know all about the other twelve Apostles—white
boys, I might add. But no mention of Rufus. And why's that?
'Cause I'm a black man. But that's just my pet peeve. I mainly
want to correct a major error that you people are basing a
faith on.

BETHANY

What's that?

RUFUS

Jesus wasn't white. Jesus was black.

RUFUS *bites into his sandwhich.* BETHANY, JAY, *and* SILENT BOB *look at him and then each other.*

JAY

Bullshit. I've seen pictures of Jesus, and He's white.

RUFUS (*wiping hands*)

That's what's particularly insulting. Between the time when He established the faith and the Church started to officially organize, the powers-that-be decided that while the message of Christ was integral, the fact that He was black was a detriment. So all renderings were ordered to be Eurocentric, even though the brother was blacker than Rudy Ray Moore.

BETHANY

If that's true, then why'd He get written about while you were left out?

RUFUS

Well, He *is* the Son of God. Kind of hard to have a New Testament without Him. So you fudge a few facts and put a spin on His ethnicity. Leaving me out is okay because you still have twelve apostles to choose from.

JAY

I don't buy it.

RUFUS

That's what the good people of Antioch were saying right before they stoned my ass.

BETHANY

You were martyred?

RUFUS

That's one way of putting it. Another way is to say I was bludgeoned to shit by big fucking rocks. Our job was to go out and spread Christ's word. I got Antioch, which was cool for awhile, because I was a big hit—they loved hearing about Jesus' message. But when I mentioned He was black, the whole town turned on me. Called me a blasphemer. I pressed the point, and before I know it, I'm playing dodgeball . . . or dodge-rock.

BETHANY

Why didn't you just let the point go when you saw how they
were reacting?

RUFUS

Because it's part of the facts. White folks only want to hear the
good shit: life eternal, a place in God's Heaven. But as soon as
they hear they're getting this good shit from a black Jesus, they
freak. And that—my friends—is called Hypocrisy. A black
man can steal your stereo, but he can't be your Savior.
(*to* SILENT BOB)
You going to eat that hash brown?

BETHANY

So you went to Heaven?

RUFUS

Well, it was the least the brother could do—in the three years
I followed His ass around Jerusalem, did I ever get laid? Hell
no! And I was in my prime. I could've been knee-deep in
shepherd's daughters, not to mention fine-ass Mary
Magdalene. She had a thing for dark meat, if you follow me.

BETHANY

Maybe this is just me talking, but if I was in Heaven, I
wouldn't care what the Bible said—as long as they got the
message right.

RUFUS

I agree—the message is what counts. But folks who build their
faith on that message should be able to disregard the color of
the skin that spoke the message. And all my rabble-rousing's
not doing much above, so I need some help down here. That's
why I'm going to help you stop those angels from getting to
that church in exchange for you helping me with my campaign.

BETHANY

How do you know about that—the angels?

RUFUS

Heaven's a pretty boring place, and anything that breaks the
tedium is news. The unmaking of existence is what you might

DOGMA 57

consider a great tedium-breaker. Besides, there isn't much I
don't know about you.

> BETHANY

I find that hard to believe.

> RUFUS

When you were five you let a kid from next door piss on
your hand.

> JAY

You did that shit? You're nasty.

> BETHANY (*shocked*)

I never told anyone about that.

> RUFUS

Neither did he. He died of leukemia two years later. His
name was . . .

> RUFUS and BETHANY

. . . Bryan Johnson.

> RUFUS

Your exploits—no matter how inane—are well-documented
in Heaven. Probably in Hell, too.

BETHANY *rubs her temples and exits oc.* RUFUS *watches her go. Jay's intrigued.*

> JAY

Yo—tell me something about me.

> RUFUS (*preoccupied with the* OC BETHANY)

You masturbate more than anyone on the planet.

> JAY

Everyone knows that. Tell me something nobody knows.

> RUFUS

When you do it, you think about guys.

RUFUS *gets up and exits.* SILENT BOB *looks at* JAY, *shocked.*

> JAY

Dude—not all the time.

BETHANY *sits on a slide in the kiddie jungle gym, shaking her head.* RUFUS
joins her.

RUFUS

I'm sorry if I spooked you.

BETHANY

I just feel . . . violated. Why does anybody care about my private bullshit? I'm just a suburban chick with a useless degree who counsels pregnant teens.

RUFUS

And Jesus was just the carpenter's kid. You've gotta face up to the fact that you're the only one who can do what has to be done here.

BETHANY

Why not get the Pope or someone holy like that?

RUFUS

Just because a guy wears a funny hat doesn't make him the right man for the job. Only certain hands can save the world from itself. The question is—are the hands attached to a person strong enough to carry the burden? I'd like to think yes.

BETHANY (*rubbing her temples*)

Two thirds of me wants to forget about this and go home. You know, yesterday I wasn't sure God even existed. And now I'm up to my ass in Christian Mythology.

RUFUS

Let me let you in on a little inside info: God *hates* it when it's referred to as mythology.

BETHANY

Well then let's ask the "prophets" what we should call it instead.

(*looking* OC; *concerned*)

Now where did those two assholes go?

INT STRIP JOINT

It's your typical strip club. One woman on a stage and a crowd of men paying way-too-much attention. The place is dimly lit with red lights and chock-

full of smoke. Off to one side, DJ *spins records, blasting the music. The crowd is rather thin.*

JAY *and* SILENT BOB *sit at the stage, bills spread out before them, their eyes glued on . . . the* DANCER—*a gorgeous, shapely vixen with very little clothing on, and growing littler by the second she smiles and starts dancing toward them.* JAY *holds up a ten-spot and performs his own little seductive dance with it. The Dancer slinks over and* JAY *stuffs the five in her G-string. She rubs his head and slinks away.* JAY *humps Silent Bob's chair, excitedly.*

Across the stage a small GANG *of bandanna-wearing, angry-looking black guys watch the* OC JAY *with little amusement. The Dancer dances toward them, but her attention is caught by some obnoxious banging on the stage. She looks to see . . .*

JAY *(flashing another ten-spot)*
Sweet thing! Look what I found!

The Dancer slinks back toward JAY *, much to the dismay of the* GANG LEADER. *His posse shake their heads at him in disappointment.*

BETHANY *and* RUFUS *come up behind* JAY *and* SILENT BOB. BETHANY *hits* JAY.

BETHANY
What are you doing?

JAY
Proving to this bastard that I ain't gay.

BETHANY
What?

RUFUS
Long story—forget it. But we should get moving. How can we get to New Jersey?

BETHANY
I had a car.

She slaps JAY *upside the head, but—riveted by the Dancer—he doesn't feel it.*

BETHANY *(to* RUFUS*)*
We'll take a train. I'll call for reservations.

RUFUS *is now also riveted—on a* TABLE DANCER *off to the side.*

> **BETHANY**
> No, it's okay. I can handle it.

RUFUS *half-nods, heading toward the other dancer.* BETHANY *shakes her head and exits.*

The Dancer is now dancing just for JAY.

The GANG LEADER *hits one of his guys, who produces a twenty dollar-bill from his jacket and casually holds it up. His posse smile and slap hands.*

The Dancer shrugs at the shocked JAY *and changes direction, heading toward the Gang.* JAY *casts a horrified look at* SILENT BOB.

The GANG LEADER *leans forward, preparing to tip when we hear an obnoxiously loud throat-clearing.*

JAY *holds aloft a fifty, smiling and nodding.*

The Dancer shrugs at the GANG LEADER *and again switches direction. The* GANG LEADER *pulls a fifty from his jacket and bangs the stage.*

In response, JAY *bangs the stage and peels off two fifties.*

Over a chorus of stage-banging, the Dancer shrugs and works the pole—letting the bidders work it out. Then, a whistling is heard. The Dancer looks over to see JAY*—standing at the stage—holding aloft three hundred-dollar bills, gyrating subtly, while sneering at the* GANG LEADER. *The Dancer joins* JAY *and grinds on him, wrapping her legs around him.* JAY *stares at the* GANG LEADER *with a victorious smirk.*

The GANG LEADER *shakes his head angrily and jumps out of his seat, producing a gun from his jacket. He fires into the ceiling. The music scratches to a halt and the other viewers scatter toward the door. The* GANG LEADER *points his piece at* JAY, *his posse backing him up.*

> **GANG LEADER**
> Alright, boy—you got at least ten seconds! And then I'm gonna cap your dumb-looking ass!

BETHANY *goes to make a move, but* RUFUS *holds her back, shaking his head.*

JAY *and* SILENT BOB *look terrified. Suddenly, they both snap into a momentary trance. Zombie-like,* JAY *and* SILENT BOB *step to the turntables behind them.* JAY *puts on headphones and begins scratching a record. A familiar tune begins.*

The Gang watches, perplexed.

SILENT BOB *whips around, microphone in his hand, and begins to sing the theme to* Fat Albert and the Cosby Kids.

JAY *rides shotgun on a nearby turntable, mixing and scratching. Both dance as they belt out a hip-hop version of that familiar cartoon staple.*

The Gang slowly goes from perplexity to enjoyment. The GANG LEADER *softens and smiles, adding a slight nod of approval.* JAY *provides backup.*

> JAY
> NOOTCH, NOOTCH, NOOTCH! KICKING IT WITH FOOD STAMPS!

> SILENT BOB
> HEY! HEY! HEY!

> JAY
> NOOTCH, NOOTCH, NOOTCH! ALL ABOUT THE PHAT CLAM!

BETHANY *and* RUFUS *look on, amazed, as*

RUFUS *makes a connection with someone OC.*

> RUFUS
> I thought she looked familiar.

> BETHANY
> Who?

> RUFUS *(he nods toward the stage)*
> Serendipity.

BETHANY *looks to the stage.*

The Dancer is the SERENDIPITY *in question. She wipes sweat from her brow and counts her earnings.*

INT. MOOBY CORP. BOARDROOM—DAY

Oh, this isn't your standard boardroom; this is Mooby Corp., home of Mooby, the Golden Calf—which can only be described as a bovine variation on a very familiar rodent-like pop icon: cartoonishly simple and very nonthreatening. A large table sits in the middle, a media center behind the huge chair at the head. The walls are adorned with framed posters of Mooby, playing with kids, mouth agape in a warm smile, surrounded by other members of the Mooby family: Surly Duck, Pat-Pat the Monkey King, etc. At the center of the table is a large, gold-plated statue of Mooby himself.

Doors open and the boardroom fills with suits—six men, one woman. They chatter and take their seats. After a beat, WHITLAND, *the* CEO, *enters, taking his place at the head of the conference table.*

> WHITLAND
>
> Good morning, shoppers.
> > (*slaps a file on table*)
> Has anyone seen the overnights?

An anticipatory hush fills the room.

> WHITLAND
>
> We creamed 'em.

A cheer and applause goes up from the group. WHITLAND *smiles.*

> WHITLAND (*reading from file*)
>
> And last night was a rerun, which says to me that with the six
> months we have to ready and promote the *Very Mooby
> Christmas* pay-per-view special, we can produce history-
> making numbers that super . . .
> > (*stops and sniffs the air*)
> Do I smell onions?

BARTLEBY *and* LOKI *sit behind the throng on a black leather couch.* LOKI *is carving something out of an onion, while* BARTLEBY *looks on.* WHITLAND *and the rest of the board stare at them.*

> WHITLAND
>
> I didn't realize we had guests. Who are these gentlemen
> with?

The other suits shrug and look to one another for an answer nobody has.

WHITLAND (*to* BARTLEBY *and* LOKI)

Excuse me.

LOKI *continues carving.* BARTLEBY *looks at his friend and shakes his head.*

LOKI (*very distracted*)

Hmm?

WHITLAND

May I ask what you're doing in my boardroom?

LOKI (*still preoccupied*)

My friend just has a few words for you, and then we'll be on our way. Um . . . this *is* corporate headquarters for Mooby Productions International, isn't it? Either that, or you guys are pretty big fans of the show.

WHITLAND

You guess correctly. Now, may I ask who the fuck you are and—again—what the fuck you're doing in my conference room?

LOKI (*to* BARTLEBY, *still not looking up*)

You may proceed, mon ami.

BARTLEBY (*to* WHITLAND)

I just want to start off by apologizing. My friend here has a bit of a penchant for the dramatic.

LOKI

(*frustrated*)

Oh, come on! You said . . .

BARTLEBY (*as if to a child*)

Relax. I'm doing it.

(*to group; circling the table*)

Mooby, the Golden Calf. Created by Nancy Goldruff—a former kindergarten teacher—in nineteen eighty-nine for local network K-REL. Bought by the Complex Corporation in nineteen ninety-one and broadcast nationally as the *The Mooby Fun-Time Hour*, it picks up a large following of children—ages three to eight. Since its inception, it has spawned sixteen records, two theatrical films, eight prime-

time specials, a library of priced-to-own videocassettes, and
bicoastal theme parks dubbed "MoobyWorld."
> (*beat*)

Did I miss anything?

WHITLAND *and company stare for a beat.*

> WHITLAND
>
> You forgot *Mooby Magazine.*

> BARTLEBY
>
> Dammit.

> WHITLAND
>
> Is there a point to this?

> BARTLEBY
>
> You and your board are idolators.

WHITLAND *and company stare dumbfounded.* LOKI *passes* BARTLEBY.

> LOKI
>
> How could you forget the magazine?

BARTLEBY *rolls his eyes.* LOKI *joins* WHITLAND *and holds up the onion
sculpture.*

> LOKI
>
> It's you.
> (*sets sculpture on table*)
> Do you know much about voodoo? It's a fascinating practice.
> No real doctrine of faith to speak of—more an arrangement of
> superstitions, the most well-known of which is the voodoo
> doll. You see . . .
> (*sneezes; waits; continues*)
> A mock-up of an individual is subjected to various pokes and
> prods. The desired result is that the individual will feel the
> effects.

> WHITLAND (*to nearest board member*)
>
> Call security—now.

LOKI *throws the knife at the table, severing the phone cord.*

> LOKI
>
> All lines are currently down.

> BARTLEBY (*to* WHITLAND)

Again—I apologize for my friend's . . .

> LOKI (*frustrated*)

Would you knock it off?!?

> BARTLEBY

Calm down.

> (*miffed; to* WHITLAND)

You are responsible for raising an icon that draws worship from the Lord. You've broken the First Commandment. But more than that, I'm afraid none of you passes for a decent human being. Your continued existence is a mockery of morality.

> (*looks to* LOKI; LOKI *nods*)

Like you—Mister Burton.

> (*stands behind board member*)

Last year you cheated on your wife of seventeen years, eight times—twice with prostitutes. You even had sex with her best friend while you were supposed to be home watching the kids.

> LOKI

In the bed you and your wife share, no less.

The board member stares in disbelief. BARTLEBY *moves on.*

> BARTLEBY

Mister Newman.

LOKI *sifts through compact discs. He pulls out one entitled "Mooby Mania" and pops it into a player. A simple children's song echoes through the room.*

> BARTLEBY

You got your girlfriend drunk at last year's Christmas party, and then paid a kid from the mailroom to have sex with her while she was passed out, just so you could break up with her—guilt free—when she sobbingly confessed the next morning. She killed herself three months later. You sent flowers to her wake.

The board member's face is frozen. BARTLEBY *shakes his head and moves quickly around the table.*

BARTLEBY

Mister Brace disowned his gay son; Mister Ray put his
mother in a third-rate nursing home and used the profits
from the sale of her house to buy an oriental rug for himself;
Mister Barker flew to the Philippines on the company account
to have sex with an eleven-year-old boy; Mister Holtzman
okayed the production of Mooby dolls from materials he
knew were toxic and unsafe because it was—survey says?

(beat)

Less costly.

BARTLEBY *stops at the female board member and looks at her, relieved.*

BARTLEBY

You, on the other hand, are an innocent. You lead a good life
and have never misused your power here. Good for you.

She stares at BARTLEBY *as he moves on.*

BARTLEBY

But you, Mister Whitland. You have more skeletons in your
closet than this assembled party. I cannot even mention them
aloud.

BARTLEBY *leans over and whispers something unheard into Whitland's ear.*
WHITLAND *goes green.* BARTLEBY *steps back.* LOKI *stands beside* WHITLAND.

LOKI

You're his father, you sick fuck.

WHITLAND *begins sobbing.*

BARTLEBY (*to* LOKI)

I think that went well.

LOKI

Yes—it did. Good job.

BARTLEBY *exits.* LOKI *turns menacingly on the others.*

LOKI

With the exception of Miss Pryce, there isn't a decent human
being amongst you. Not one. Do you know what makes a
human being decent?

(*beat*)

Fear. And therein lies the problem. None of you has anything left to fear anymore. You rest comfortably in seats of inscrutable power, hiding behind your false idol, far from judgment—lives shrouded in secrecy even from one another. But not from God.

LOKI *goes to exit but pauses. He turns around.*

LOKI

I forgot my little voodoo doll.

(*looks at* WHITLAND)

Wow. It really does look just like you. Maybe, if I believed enough . . . I wonder . . .

LOKI *begins moaning menacingly, slowly waving an open palm over the figure.* WHITLAND *looks at it horrified, then at* LOKI, *then back at the figure. He sweats and shifts in his seat—eyes pinned on the figure.* LOKI *lets out a shriek and smashes the figure with his fist.* WHITLAND *freezes, eyes closed. Slowly, he opens his eyes—unharmed.*

LOKI

I don't believe in voodoo.

LOKI *swiftly exits. The board members sit in awed silence. Then the doors burst open and* LOKI *storms back in.*

LOKI

But I do believe in this.

He jumps atop the boardroom table and marches down its length. Gun blazing, he takes out the male board members, including WHITLAND, *in a flurry of bullets.*

EXT BOARDROOM—SAME

BARTLEBY *sits on a couch, reading a magazine, listening to the hail of bullets. He shakes his head.*

BARTLEBY (*as* LOKI)

"I do believe in this." What does that mean?

INT MOOBY CORP. BOARDROOM—SAME

The remaining female board member covers her head with her arms. LOKI
helps her to her feet.

> LOKI
>
> Gum?

He offers her a stick of his gum. Scared, she takes it.

> LOKI *(smiling)*
>
> It's okay. You've done nothing wrong. Those guys were bad
> men. You're a pure soul.

She looks at him, terrified. He smiles back. Then his expression hardens.

> LOKI
>
> But you didn't say "God Bless You" when I sneezed.

He quickly puts the gun to her head. She slams her eyes shut.

> OC BARTLEBY *(cautionary)*
>
> Loki!

LOKI *freezes and looks OC. He deflates.*

> LOKI *(to* WOMAN*)*
>
> You're getting off light!

> OC BARTLEBY
>
> Loki!

> LOKI
>
> I'm coming.
>
> *(to* WOMAN*)*
>
> You're so lucky.

*He grabs his knife and exits. The female board member slowly opens her eyes
and looks around.*

INT STRIP JOINT—LATER

JAY *and the* GANG LEADER *sit together at a table, surrounded by the other
gangsters and* SILENT BOB. *They laugh and chug their 40s.*

> GANG LEADER
>
> Do it again, G. Do the Mush-mouth.

JAY (*swigs his beer; as ìMush-mouthî*)
Hey-buh, Fat-buh, Al-buh-bert.

The Gang laughs hysterically.

GANGSTER 1
Fat Albert like a motherfucker and shit!

BETHANY, RUFUS, *and* SERENDIPITY *huddle around a table farther away.*

RUFUS (*elated*)
I forgot you were down here! How long now?

SERENDIPITY
Three years this August. What about you—is this another
temporary expulsion? You and your "Christ was down"
campaign?

BETHANY
What does that mean—another expulsion? I thought you
came down here specifically to help me?

SERENDIPITY
Is that what he told you? Rufus gets thrown out constantly; at
least once a month, ethereal time. They always bring him
back, but only after a few days of peace and quiet—free from
that black nationalist rhetoric.

RUFUS
Artsy-fartsy bitch . . .

SERENDIPITY
Who you calling artsy-fartsy?

RUFUS
Serendipity here used to hang with us sometimes back in
Jerusalem.

BETHANY
Let me guess—the fourteenth apostle; left out of the Bible
because she's a woman.

RUFUS
This girl's not a woman.
(*to* SERENDIPITY)
No offense.

BETHANY

Oh, those weren't tits I saw Jay cozying up to?

SERENDIPITY (*tugs on boobs*)

What, these? You should know better than anyone at this table that tits don't make a woman.

RUFUS

Hell, the tubby, coat-wearing motherfucker's got tits—don't make him a woman.

SERENDIPITY

Aside from an intuitive knack for accessorizing, what traditionally defines a woman falls between two things: her legs. But as you can see . . .

SERENDIPITY *stands and unbuttons her jeans, dropping them slightly, revealing yet another smooth, sexless crotch, quite like Metatron's.*

SERENDIPITY

. . . I lack definition.

OC JAY

Hey! They're getting a free show!

SERENDIPITY *pulls her pants back up and sits down, smiling at the OC party.*

BETHANY (*weary*)

Oh God. Another angel. Like Metatron.

SERENDIPITY

How do you know Metatron?

(*to* RUFUS)

How does she know Metatron?

RUFUS

This is the Last Scion.

SERENDIPITY (*beat*)

You're kidding. Wow.

RUFUS

Don't you see the resemblance?

SERENDIPITY

A bit.

(*suddenly nervous*)

Oh shit. If she's been tapped, then something's up.

BETHANY

I'm confused.

RUFUS

Bethany, Serendipity here isn't technically an angel, nor is she by any means a human being like I was and you are.

SERENDIPITY

Amen to that.

(*swigs her beer and spits it out*)

BETHANY

Then who is she?

SERENDIPITY

Not who—what. I haven't always been part of the anthropomorphic club. I used to be an abstract.

BETHANY

Now I'm really confused.

RUFUS

Serendipity's an idea.

SERENDIPITY

Try *all* ideas.

BETHANY

Meaning?

SERENDIPITY

I'm a muse, stupid.

BETHANY *stares at her for a beat, then at* RUFUS. RUFUS *nods affirmatively.*

BETHANY

I can't take much more of this.

(*downs her beer*)

RUFUS (*to* SERENDIPITY)

She's now met a seraphim, a dead man, and a muse. You can appreciate her frame of mind.

BETHANY (*to* SERENDIPITY)

So you—what—inspire people?

SERENDIPITY

What just went down with your friends over there—you
don't think they thought of that themselves? I knew Kane's
weak spot for Fat Albert and passed it along to the boys.

RUFUS

If she hadn't interceded, they'd be chalk lines right now.

BETHANY

You made them sing that song?

SERENDIPITY

I offered them a solution out of the hole they dug for
themselves. Thankfully, they took it.

BETHANY

Are you kidding? Those two are so dense, they wouldn't get
a good idea if it was given to them in a specially marked box.

SERENDIPITY

Dense people are the most open to suggestion—it's you so-
called intelligent folks that have a hard time accepting a good
idea.

RUFUS

Ain't that the truth.

BETHANY

Prove it. Give me a good idea.

SERENDIPITY

If I do, and you accept it, then you'll have confirmation that
you are—as you say—dense.

BETHANY (*beat*)

Alright. So you're a muse. So what kind of people do you
inspire—besides stupid ones?

SERENDIPITY

I used to specialize in entertainment—literature, theatre, so
forth. Then for awhile it was the movies.

BETHANY

Which ones?

SERENDIPITY

Off the top of my head—everything. Well, almost everything.
For example: I'm responsible for nineteen of the twenty top-
grossing films of all time.

BETHANY

Nineteen?

SERENDIPITY

The one about the kid, by himself in his house; burglars
trying to get in and he fights them off?
(BETHANY *nods*)
I had nothing to do with that one. Somebody sold their soul
to Satan to get the grosses up on that piece of shit.

RUFUS

Which brings us to the next logical question—what are you
doing stripping?

SERENDIPITY

Well, you remember why I left, right?

RUFUS

You were tired of doing all the work and getting none of the
credit for your ideas.

SERENDIPITY

And sick of watching incapable people take brilliant
inspiration and turn out real trash. So I opted to quit being a
muse and write for myself. I gave my two weeks' notice, got a
body, fifty bucks, and got sent out into the world to make my
fortune.

BETHANY

So what happened?

SERENDIPITY

Writer's block. Can you believe it? Me—a muse, for God's
sake!

BETHANY

What about what you did with Jay and Silent Bob?

SERENDIPITY

That's the cosmic joke. I can inspire anyone I meet, and give out a zillion and nine ideas a second, but I can't keep any for myself. Her quirky sense of humor.

BETHANY

Whose?

SERENDIPITY

God's.

BETHANY

You're saying God's a woman.

SERENDIPITY

Was there ever a doubt in your mind?

BETHANY

The possibility never presented itself. He's always referred to as a Him.

SERENDIPITY

That's not how I wrote it. But one of the drawbacks to being intangible is that you have no say in the editorial process. My job stopped at the inspirational whisper stage—the people that held the pens added their own perspective. And all the pen-holders were men. So She became a He. Doesn't stop with God, either—the whole book is gender-biased: a woman's responsible for original sin, a woman cuts Samson's coif of power, a woman asks for the head of John the Baptist. Read that book again sometime—women are painted as bigger antagonists than the Egyptians and Romans combined. It stinks.

INT STRIP CLUB BATHROOM

A toilet flushes as a man exits a stall. The toilet overflows, and the water it spills turns from clear to murky brown, then to thick shit, which spreads across the floor.

INT STRIP CLUB

BETHANY, SERENDIPITY, *and* RUFUS *continue their discussion.*

BETHANY (*stunned*)
God is a woman . . .

SERENDIPITY
I don't know what the big surprise is. Read you psychology—
it's theorized that since a female can give birth to and nurture
both sexes, women are the only gender both sexes can feel
completely comfortable with. Don't the faithful—both male
and female—feel the same way about God? In time of trial, our
first instinct is to implore the aid of the Almighty, just as when
you're a child, the only person who can make it all better is . . .

BETHANY
. . . mom. God, it makes sense.

RUFUS (*to* SERENDIPITY)
Shit, you still have a knack for words.

SERENDIPITY
Not really useful in my new line of work.

RUFUS
I gotta say it again—*stripping?!?*

SERENDIPITY
Oh, shut up, you—I was trying to create something artistic I
could call my own! If you third-leggers could look beyond
these . . .

(grabs tits)

. . . you'd notice that we do more than take off our clothes up
on that stage. It's dancing——and while it's not the great
ethereal novel, it *is* a form of artistic expression, right? Well, I
figured I could live with that. But She won't even give me
that much. The way God designed dance, it's one of the only
creative acts which results in no tangible product. You paint,
you got a painting; you write lyrics, you got a song. But you
dance? When the dance is over, there's nothing to show for
it—nothing to save and enjoy . . . or sell. So I'm back to square
one. Ah—at least the tips are good . . . You just have to put up
with a lot of shit.

INT STRIP CLUB BATHROOOM

The shit pouring out of the toilet begins forming into an anthropomorphic form.

INT STRIP CLUB

BETHANY, SERENDIPITY, *and* RUFUS *continue.*

> RUFUS
>
> Didn't I always tell you—having a body ain't all it's cracked up to be.

> SERENDIPITY
>
> Why didn't I listen? I can't stand being flesh anymore, especially this halfway crap. Not only do I have to take care of the aesthetic—the showers, the hair-cutting, the pit-shaving—but I can't take advantage of the benefits: like getting laid or using my period as an excuse not to get laid . . .
>
> (*conspiratorily to* BETHANY)
>
> . . . the only true boon to having a period, from what I understand. Excuse me.
>
> (*to* RUFUS)
>
> Why's the Last Scion here?

> RUFUS
>
> Bartleby and Loki?

> SERENDIPITY
>
> Sure—the Angel of Death and his squeamish pal with a conscience.

> RUFUS
>
> They found a way back.

> SERENDIPITY (*shocked*)
>
> God, no. Not the plenary indulgence loophole?

> BETHANY
>
> You know about that?

> SERENDIPITY
>
> I always knew that thing was a bad idea. Leave it to the Catholics to destroy existence.

BETHANY

You've got issues with Catholicism, I take it?

SERENDIPITY

I've got issues with anyone who treats God like a burden instead of a blessing—like some Catholics. You people don't celebrate your faith—you mourn it.

BETHANY

So if we're wrong, then what's the right religion?

SERENDIPITY

When are you people going to learn? It's not about who's right or wrong. No denomination's nailed it yet, and they never will because they're all too self-righteous to realize that it doesn't matter what you have faith in—just that you *have* faith. Your hearts are in the right place, but your brains have to wake up.

INT STRIP CLUB BATHROOM

Tight on the "head" of the massive form, as an eye widely opens. Something growls.

INT STRIP CLUB

JAY *and* SILENT BOB *race up to the table, wearing bandannas.*

JAY

They made me and Silent Bob part of the gang!

Suddenly, the bathroom door blows open. The massive shit-formed FIGURE *stands in the doorway. The light and vapors surrounding him are brown.*

FIGURE (*deep, guttural hiss*)

Not born . . . shit into existence.

Our group stares at the OC brute. JAY *sniffs the air.*

JAY

Who fucking farted?

SERENDIPITY

Sweet Christ, someone wants you bad.

> BETHANY

What is that thing?!

> SERENDIPITY

An excremental—the Golgothan.

> JAY

A what?

> RUFUS

A shit-demon.

The Golgothan moves slowly from the door, toward the group.

> NO-MAN

No . . . man . . . of . . . woman . . . born . . .

The Gang join the others. They hold and cover their noses while drawing weapons.

> GANG LEADER

Friend of yours?

> JAY (*to group*)

Is this smelly fuck with us?

> RUFUS

He came for Bethany!

> JAY (*to* GANG LEADER)

Smoke that motherfucker like it ain't no thang!

> GANG LEADER

I knew I'd get to wax someone today. Represent!

The Gang charges OC, guns blazing, while we hold on the group. Suddenly, the room is filled with screams and wet, slurpy noises. The noise stops, and the group reacts.

The Gang lays about NO-MAN, *dead, covered in murky, creamy crap—their wide eyes frozen in horror.* NO-MAN *scoops a fingerful of the muck into his mouth, smiling.*

Our heroes start backing up slowly, as not to be noticed.

> JAY (*to* SILENT BOB)

I guess we're in charge of the gang now.

SERENDIPITY

Go for the bar!

They dash. NO-MAN *snaps to attention and throws its arm at them, launching a huge glob of shit through the air.*

JAY (*looking back; panicked*)

SHIT!!!!

Everyone leaps behind the bar. The shit flies over them and slams into the wall behind the bar, destroying it.

JAY

Where'd that thing come from?

SERENDIPITY

You ever hear of Golgotha?

BETHANY

Skull place. The hill where Christ was crucified.

SERENDIPITY

Yeah, well it wasn't just Christ up there—the Romans crucified everybody on that hill. And Christ excluded, they were all criminals—killers, brigands, thieves, rapists. And whenever the crucified expired, their bodies would naturally lose muscle control, spilling bowel and bladder in the process, the result of which is that walking pile of crap up there: the Golgothan Shit-Demon—Hell's chief assassin. And it's here for you, girlie.

Something occurs to SILENT BOB. *He steps out from behind the bar.*

BETHANY

Bob, get down!

JAY

You tubby retard! Get your ass back here!

SILENT BOB *stands like a statue in the Golgothan's path. The demon snarls a smile, moving ever closer.* SILENT BOB *reaches into his coat and pulls a small canister out. He points it at the beast. A mist sprays into the face of the Golgothan. It pauses, looking confused, then drops to the floor.*

BETHANY, RUFUS, SERENDIPITY, *and* JAY *crowd around* SILENT BOB *, staring at the fallen unconscious behemoth. They then look to* SILENT BOB *and the canister in his hand.*

> BETHANY

How?

He hands the canister to BETHANY. *It's a small, trial-size can of air freshener.*

> BETHANY (*reading can*)

"Knocks strong odors out."

> RUFUS

Way to go, tubby.

> BETHANY

Why would you ever carry this?

JAY *farts.* SILENT BOB *sprays the freshener at his ass. The others look at* JAY.

> JAY

What?!

> RUFUS

Can you squeeze this thing for some answers?

> SERENDIPITY

I can give it a shot.

> BETHANY

What's going on?

> RUFUS

The Muse is going to talk to that demon.

> JAY

Cool! Can we watch?

> SERENDIPITY

Not a good idea. Demons can wreak havoc on the weak-minded.

> JAY

Fuck you—weak-minded! Me and Silent Bob can talk to him in his own language! See . . . ?
>   (*makes the universal metal sign*)
> He'd understand this.

SERENDIPITY (*shakes her head; to* RUFUS)

Whoever sent this might send more. I suggest you take the princess and get as far away as possible. I'll do what I can to get something out of poopie-boy here. If there's anything helpful, I'll get it to you somehow.

BETHANY (*hugs her*)

Thank you. And . . . you're a great dancer.

SERENDIPITY

You should see me juggle.

(*to* JAY *and* SILENT BOB)

Hey. You know you're supposed to be prophets, right? Then start acting like prophets. You should have seen that thing coming.

JAY

Why the hell are we getting yelled at?!

SERENDIPITY

Just watch out for Bethany. Go.

BETHANY *leads* JAY *and* SILENT BOB *out of the bar.*

JAY

Man, bitch thinks just 'cause she's good-looking, she can tell us what to do.

BETHANY

She told me that if you behave, she'd sleep with you.

JAY (*excited*)

Yeah?!

BETHANY

Oh, a demon'd have a field day with you.

SERENDIPITY *and* RUFUS *watch them disappear up the steps.*

OC JAY

Shut up.

OC BETHANY

You shut up.

SERENDIPITY (*to* RUFUS)

Nice girl.

                            RUFUS
Comes from good stock.

                         SERENDIPITY
You haven't told her yet?

                            RUFUS
Not the right time.

                         SERENDIPITY
How uncanny is the resemblance? Those eyes, the lips . . .

                            RUFUS
The nails.

SERENDIPITY *looks at* RUFUS. *He smiles. She hits him.*

                         SERENDIPITY
Blasphemer.

Then, the OC Golgothan makes a groggy, grumbling noise.

                         SERENDIPITY
Shit. You'd better go. I'll take care of the trash.

                        RUFUS (*hugs her*)
Good luck.

RUFUS *exits.* SERENDIPITY *turns to the Golgothan.*

                         SERENDIPITY
Alright, Stinky—let's see what you know.

INSERT T.V. NEWS FOOTAGE

There's a throng of people outside the Vatican. Cut to a shot of the "Buddy-Christ" being installed in the main altar. Camera flashes pop.

                         VOICE-OVER
And today in Vatican City, the "Buddy-Christ" was officially
installed on the main altar of Saint Peter's Basilica, to scores
of both cheers and protests. Pope John Paul the Second has
urged the faithful to have patience with the subtle changes
the centuries-old religion is undergoing, indicating that he
found the new symbol of Christ to be "hip."

INT BUS TERMINAL—DAY

The visual of the "Buddy-Christ" with his thumb up is captured on a monitor in a bus terminal. BARTLEBY *and* LOKI *stare up at it, then turn toward the ticket window.*

> LOKI

And you say Siskel and Ebert have no influence over this culture.

> BARTLEBY (*to* WOMAN *in window*)

We'd like two tickets to New Jersey, please.

> WOMAN

Jersey's sold out, sir.

> LOKI

What?! Come on—how many people can possibly be going to New Jersey?

> WOMAN

Enough to fill a bus. There's another one the same time tomorrow. I suggest you not underestimate the staggering drawing power of the Garden State and show up two hours in advance.

> (*closes window*)

> BARTLEBY

Nice. Your hard-on for smiting has prevented us from negotiating what should be the relatively simple matter of catching or staying on a bus!

> LOKI

Ah, bus-shmus. Besides—why should we fall victim to gravity when we can just as easily rise above?

> BARTLEBY (*stares at him*)

Fly?

> LOKI

We got wings, right? Fuck—let's use them!

> OC VOICE

I wouldn't suggest that.

The pair spin and gawk.

AZRAEL *leans in the doorway. He removes his hat, revealing two stubby horns.*

> AZRAEL
>
> You wouldn't want to look like a couple of fairies, now would you?

EXT SOMEWHERE IN LIMBO

Vast whiteness, in the middle of which sits a puddle of half-formed No-Man. SERENDIPITY *draws a circle around it with lipstick. Once finished, she leans in close to it.*

> SERENDIPITY
>
> Voulez-vous coucher avec moi, ce soir?

NO-MAN *wakens violently.* SERENDIPITY *backs up. It settles down and sees her.*

> NO-MAN
>
> The Muse.

> SERENDIPITY
>
> No-Man.

> NO-MAN (*taking in surroundings*)
>
> Where have you taken us?

> SERENDIPITY
>
> Well, I didn't know what I was going to tell the cops when they showed up, so I brought us to Limbo. Figured this was as good a place as any to chat with you.

> NO-MAN
>
> Is this . . . Paradise?

> SERENDIPITY
>
> Limbo? God no. It's a place the Catholic Church made up. Where babies that hadn't been baptised supposedly went. They've since scrapped the notion and desanctified the place. I come here sometimes—when I need to get away . . . or tie up shit-demons.
> (*beat*)
> Got some questions for you, No-Man.

> NO-MAN
>
> Free us from the binding circle . . . that you may have answers.

> SERENDIPITY (*heads toward it*)

Okay.

> (*stops; sarcastic*)

Oh wait—I'm smarter than that.

NO-MAN *lets out a bellow.*

> SERENDIPITY

This can go hard or easy. The sooner I get what I want, the sooner you'll be free. Now, you can start by telling me what you were doing on the mortal plane?

> NO-MAN (*beat*)

Liquidate the Last Scion.

> SERENDIPITY

See? That wasn't so hard. Now—who sent you? Was it Lucifer?

NO-MAN *laughs in a sinister fashion.*

> NO-MAN

The Morningstar has grown weak in his complacency . . . his mandate holds dominion over us no longer.

> SERENDIPITY

So how are you here, then? Did you escape?

> NO-MAN

No soul escapes Hell but one . . . our Master . . . who is come to sever reality and crush existence . . . as a thumb punctures a fontanel . . . bringing calm for those who've perdition suffered.

> SERENDIPITY

So you've got a *new* boss—Bartleby and Loki, perhaps?

> NO-MAN

Resist no further, Muse. Deliver unto us the conflicted splinter of Divinity, that the waking world may unravel, or know your efforts fruitless only as being becomes not, and the abandoned cognize that the God of Abraham lay dormant while the dream perished in a blink.

SERENDIPITY

Stop trying to be so spooky. Tell me who sent you, or I'll use whatever influence I have below to make Hell even worse for you.

NO-MAN

You speak of Azrael as if the flames still cage him.

SERENDIPITY

What do you mean? Are you saying he's gone?

NO-MAN *snaps to attention, as if it's heard something. It then glares at* SERENDIPITY.

NO-MAN

Would that I could cross the threshold of your confining circle, I would crush your half-life throat. But my Master does not abandon me to this mockery of a prison. We will come back for the girl. And when we do, it will take more than fragrant mist to keep our hands from crushing her head.

NO-MAN *goes stiff, and then limp. His body begins to melt.*

SERENDIPITY

TELL ME WHO SENT YOU, DEMON!!!

But it's gone, leaving only a huge puddle of shit. SERENDIPITY *deflates, frustrated.*

SERENDIPITY

Shit.

INT TOY STORE—DAY

AZRAEL *leads* BARTLEBY *and* LOKI *through the aisles, passing tons of stuffed animals.*

BARTLEBY

Look at this pimp. How'd you get out of Hell?

AZRAEL

I told them I was coming up on a routine possession. I don't have much time. If they figure out my ruse, they'll come looking for me.

BARTLEBY

You lied?

LOKI

Go figure. Him. A demon.

(*to* AZRAEL)

What's with bringing us in here?

AZRAEL

Because you two fucks are inches away from getting caught.
Going around killing people, about to uncase your wings . . .
don't you have any idea what's going on?

BARTLEBY

We're going home.

AZRAEL

Oh really? Are you so clueless as to think you can just waltz
back into Heaven?

BARTLEBY

Why not? We're going back clean.

AZRAEL

Let me let you in on a little secret, pal: everyone is looking for
you. Both sides—above and below. The orders are to
terminate you on sight.

BARTLEBY (*shocked*)

Why?

AZRAEL

Because you're pissing people off, that's why! Word on the
grapevine is that God's pissed off at your presumption, and I
know Lucifer's pissed because you assholes might make him
look bad, by succeeding where he's failed so many times.

BARTLEBY

So they're going to kill us?!?

AZRAEL

They're gonna try. That's why you have to travel incognito—
tone down your behavior, stay off their respective radars.
Quit killing people—that's high profile. And for God's sake,
don't uncase your wings until you have to transubstantiate.

Because the minute you do, legions of thrones and hordes of
demons will fight each other over who gets to kill you first.
                        (*looks OC*)
Shhhh!

A WOMAN *and her small* DAUGHTER *walk past. While the Woman looks at
the items on the top shelf,* LOKI *pulls off Azrael's hat and taps the* DAUGH-
TER *on the shoulder. He points to Azrael's horns. The Woman pulls the*
DAUGHTER *farther down the aisle, oblivious to the trio.*

                        DAUGHTER
Mommy, that man had horns!

AZRAEL *grabs his hat and puts it back on, as* LOKI *chuckles.*

                        AZRAEL
See? Now that's the kind of shit I'm talking about!

                        LOKI
Oh, lighten up.

                BARTLEBY (*still reeling*)
I can't believe they want to kill us.

                        AZRAEL
Believe it, boys. They've even got the Last Scion looking for
you.

                        LOKI
You're kidding!

                        AZRAEL
This is big, man. Your reentry is a thorn in a lot of sides, and
they'll stop at nothing—I mean *nothing*—to prevent it.

                        LOKI
If that's the case, then why are you helping us?

                        AZRAEL
Because you were both given a raw deal—almost as raw as
mine. And if you make it back, then I figure there's hope for
me.
                        (*looks around*)
In the meantime, I suggest you find an alternate mode of
transportation. If anything else comes up, I'll contact you.

> BARTLEBY

Thank you, Azrael. You're a true friend.

> AZRAEL

Would you expect anything less from a demon? I have to get back to the Pit, before they get suspicious. And remember: incognito.

AZRAEL *turns to leave.*

> LOKI

Hey, Az—is it as bad down there as they say?

> AZRAEL

Give you a hint: they've been playing *Mrs. Doubtfire* continuously for the last five years.

> (*exits*)

> LOKI

Shit, man—that *is* punishment.

EXT CONTRYSIDE—NIGHT

The train chugs through the darkness.

INT TRAIN—NIGHT

BETHANY *and* RUFUS *sit across from one another. They stare out the window.*

> RUFUS

How you coping, kid?

> BETHANY

It's weird. Just when I think I've got a handle on things, something wholly unbelievable presents itself. Sometimes I wish I had just stayed home.

> RUFUS

You sound like the Man.

> BETHANY (*beat*)

What's He like?

> RUFUS

Jesus? Black.

BETHANY

Besides that.

RUFUS

He likes to hear people talk. Says it sounds like music to Him.
Christ loved to sit around the fire and listen to me and the
other guys. Whenever we were going on about unimportant
shit, He always had a smile on His face.

BETHANY

Maybe because not having anything of value to say was a
luxury He was never granted.

RUFUS

Could be, could be. But He *is* a booster, though—always pulling
for humanity. He calls us His alma mater. His only real beef
with mankind is the shit that gets carried out in His name—
wars, bigotry, televangelism. The *big* one, though, is the
factioning of all the religions. He said humanity got it all wrong
by taking a good idea and building a belief structure on it.

BETHANY

You're saying that having beliefs is a bad thing?

RUFUS

I think it's better to have ideas. You can change an idea.
Changing a belief is trickier. Life should be malleable, but
beliefs anchor you to certain points and limit growth—new
ideas can't generate and life becomes stagnant. That's
something else that bugs Christ—still life. He wants everyone
to be as enthralled with living as He was. The Man loved
being human—probably why He was so good at it. You know
He was the only person I've ever known that *never* engaged
in that most time-honored of all the life-affirming activities.

BETHANY

Sex.

RUFUS

Debate. That's the only way most folks know how to confirm
they're alive. People spend their whole lives debating: we
fight about who's right and who's wrong, we fight ourselves,
we fight death, we fight over beliefs, we fight over fights. It's

as if we think that to stop debating—in any fashion—is to stop being vital. I'm even guilty of it myself, the way I go on about the issue of Christ's ethnicity, always fighting for the truth to be told. And I'm dead. Even in death, the only way I know how to live is through debate. That's sad, isn't it?

BETHANY

Not if you believe it's important for people to know.

RUFUS

A belief's a dangerous thing, Bethany. People die for it. People kill for it. The whole of existence is in jeopardy right now because of the Catholic belief structure regarding this plenary indulgence bullshit. And Bartleby and Loki—whether they know it or not—are exploiting that belief, and if they're successful, you, me, all of this . . . ends in a heartbeat. All over a belief.

BETHANY *nods.* RUFUS *looks around.*

RUFUS

I haven't seen the moron twins in awhile. How about you?

BETHANY

They went to the lounge car to smoke.
(*getting up*)
I'll go find them; make sure they're not getting into any trouble.

BETHANY *heads off.* RUFUS *looks out the window, then shuts his eyes.*

INT LOUNGE CAR—NIGHT

BETHANY *enters and spots* JAY *and* SILENT BOB, *talking to an unseen party.*

BETHANY

You two aren't getting into any trouble, are you?

JAY

Hell no. Just about to smoke a bowl with our new friends that just got on at the last stop.

SILENT BOB *moves over, revealing the new friends.* BARTLEBY *and* LOKI *smile at* BETHANY.

> JAY

This is Larry and Barry.

> LOKI

Jay tells us you're going to sleep with him.

EXT TRAIN TRACKS—NIGHT

The train rushes overhead.

INT LOUNGE CAR—LATER

LOKI, JAY, *and* SILENT BOB *pass a joint under the table and take quick hits, trying to remain casual.* JAY *pounds the table happily.*

BARTLEBY *and* BETHANY *lie on either side of the table in their booth.*

> BETHANY

You can smoke up with them if you want. You don't have to keep me company.

> BARTLEBY

It's a long trip. There'll be plenty of time later.
> (*beat*)
So why are you heading to Jersey?

> BETHANY

There's just this thing there I've gotta do. You?

> BARTLEBY

We're going home.

> BETHANY

Do you two live together?

> BARTLEBY

Unfortunately. Do you live with those guys?

> BETHANY

God, no. They just sort of adopted me.

> BARTLEBY

They're funny. The big one never says a word.

> BETHANY

I wish the little one would take a cue from him.

BARTLEBY

Lo . . . Larry's taken an immediate shine to them.

BETHANY

How long've you two been together?

BARTLEBY

Awhile. He can be a little flaky sometimes, but we've got a lot in common.

BETHANY

How'd you meet?

BARTLEBY

We were stationed together.

BETHANY

See? That's beautiful. And everyone's always up-in-arms about this "out-in-the-military" issue.

BARTLEBY

Pardon?

BETHANY

Well there's all that macho bullshit about it being "This Man's Army," and you two meet there and hook up, which proves that love blooms where it—

BARTLEBY

You think we're lovers?! Oh no. No, we're not gay.

BETHANY

Oh God, I'm sorry! I just assumed . . .

BARTLEBY

No. We live together and all, but at the end of the night, I go to my room, and he goes to his.
(*beat*)
Why? Do I come off as gay?

BETHANY (*laughing*)

No, not at all. My ex-husband kind of screwed up my relationship awareness barometer.

BARTLEBY

You're divorced?

BETHANY
That's a nice way of putting it. I call it being dumped.

BARTLEBY
I was dumped once. More or less.

BETHANY
It's terrible, isn't it? Don't you constantly question your value—like why was I so easy to cast aside?

BARTLEBY
And you wonder if the other party's going to come to their senses and call you back.

BETHANY
The worst is that I still think like a couple. After all these years, I still have the "we" mentality.

BARTLEBY
Mine grew out of one of those misunderstandings that results in a communication breakdown. And then I realized I was abandoned. Then it hits you—"I was replaced by someone." A lot of someones.

BETHANY
And they always tell you it'll hurt less with time . . .

BARTLEBY
. . . when actually, it hurts more.

BETHANY (*beat*)
You know what we need? We need drinks. A lot of drinks.

INT TRAIN CAR—NIGHT

RUFUS *continues to slumber, using his shoe as a pillow.*

INT LOUNGE CAR—NIGHT

JAY *is asleep on Silent Bob's shoulder, drooling slightly.* LOKI *talks with* SILENT BOB.

LOKI
I'm telling you, man—it's all about organized religion and society's battle against it. The Rebels are fighting the Empire,

right? Now the Empire is led by whom? Darth Vader? No. It's led by the Emperor. And the Emperor is a practitioner of the Force, albeit the Dark Side of the Force. And the Force is basically a religion.

(SILENT BOB *nods*)

So the entire galaxy is under Imperial rule, and the Imperial government is run by this old religion. What you have, then, is a theocracy—a government run by the church. So Luke, Han, and Leia are fighting that government to liberate the galaxy from the pious grip of what is, in essence, Holy Mother Church.

SILENT BOB *nods in understanding.*

BETHANY *and* BARTLEBY *slump in their booth, the table loaded with empty glasses.* BETHANY *is quite tipsy.* BARTLEBY *hasn't touched his booze.*

BARTLEBY

You're saying you still go to church?

BETHANY (*laughs*)

Every Sunday.

BARTLEBY

Does it do anything for you?

BETHANY (*thinks*)

Gives me time to balance my checkbook every week.

BARTLEBY

See? That's what I'm talking about. People don't go to church and feel spiritual. They go to church and feel bored. But they keep going. Every week. Out of habit.

BETHANY

Or in habit, if you're a nun.

(*starts laughing*)

I'm sorry—that was *bad*! I am *so* buzzed.

BARTLEBY

When do you think you lost your faith?

BETHANY

Oh, I remember the exact moment. I was on the phone with my mother, and she was trying to counsel me through this . . .

this thing. And at one point, when nothing she was saying was making me feel any better, she said, "Bethany—God has a plan." And I . . . I just got so angry. I was like "What about *my* plans?" You know? Don't they count for anything? I had planned to have a family with my husband—wasn't that plan good enough for God?

(*beat*)

Apparently not.

(*swigs her drink*)

How about you? When did you lose your faith?

BARTLEBY

Me? Years ago. One day, God just stopped listening. I kept talking, but I got the distinct impression that He wasn't listening anymore.

BETHANY

She. And how do you know She was listening in the first place?

BARTLEBY (*thinks*)

I guess I don't.

BETHANY

I hate thoughts like that. But they occur to you with age. When you're a kid, you never question the whole faith thing—God's in Heaven, and He's . . . She's always got Her eye on you. I'd give anything to feel that way again. I guess that's why I let myself get talked into this pilgrimage.

BARTLEBY

Where's this pilgrimage to?

INT TRAIN CAR—NIGHT

RUFUS *stirs. He looks around and stretches.*

INT LOUNGE CAR—NIGHT

BETHANY *and* BARTLEBY *continue their discussion.*

BETHANY

You'd never believe me if I told you.

                    BARTLEBY
Try me.

                    BETHANY
Alright. But I warned you. Okay—I'm going to this church in
New Jersey.

                    BARTLEBY
Really . . .

INT TRAIN CAR—NIGHT

RUFUS *heads toward the back of the car. He opens the door between the cars and exits.*

INT LOUNGE CAR—NIGHT

BETHANY *and* BARTLEBY *talk further. Bartleby's intrigued.*

                    BETHANY
I'm supposed to stop a couple of angels from entering the
church. They're trying . . .
                    (*laughing*)
This sounds so stupid . . . They're trying to get back into
Heaven!

INT TRAIN CAR—NIGHT

RUFUS *passes through another car and opens the door at the end.*

INT LOUNGE CAR—NIGHT

BARTLEBY *grows very tense.* BETHANY *rattles on, half-toasted.*

                    BETHANY
See, they got tossed out of Heaven years ago, right? And if
they get back in, it proves God wrong. And since God is
infallible, to prove Her wrong would . . .
                    (*laughing hard*)
. . . would unmake existence! I feel so stupid just saying it.

Bartleby's eyes are wide. He looks scared. Then, a calm falls over him.

BETHANY

But the thing I don't get . . . is how do I stop an angel? Two, even! I guess I'm supposed to talk them out of it or something.

As BETHANY *laughs,* BARTLEBY *surreptitiously slides a knife off the table.*

BARTLEBY

Maybe you're supposed to kill them?

BETHANY *breaks into hysterics.*

INT TRAIN CAR—NIGHT

RUFUS *is stopped by a porter who checks his ticket.*

INT LOUNGE CAR—NIGHT

Bethany's still cracking up, oblivious to the on-the-defensive BARTLEBY.

BETHANY

Oh yeah! Right! Kill them! Even if that was the case—which it's not—I mean, how do you kill an angel, Barry?

BARTLEBY

I don't suppose it's much different . . .
                    (*slowly lifts the knife*)
. . . from killing a human . . .

The door behind them slides open. RUFUS *steps in.*

RUFUS

Where the hell is everybody? I wake up, and . . .

He sees BARTLEBY. *They both freeze.*

BARTLEBY

The Apostle!

RUFUS

Holy shit!

BETHANY (*stumbling to her feet*)

Rufus, I want you to meet my friend, Barry . . .

BARTLEBY *leaps out of the booth and grabs* BETHANY, *holding the knife to her throat.*

> BETHANY (*chuckling*)
>
> Don't be such a show-off, Barry!

> RUFUS
>
> Take it easy, Bartleby. Just let her go and we can talk about this.

> BETHANY (*realizing*)
>
> Bartleby?!

> BARTLEBY
>
> So this is what it comes down to, Rufus—after all this time? Slaughtered by this meat puppet!

> BETHANY
>
> Take your fucking hands off me, you dickless sonovabitch!

> BARTLEBY
>
> Save it, lady—five minutes ago, you were aching to top me off!
> (*calling over shoulder*)
>
> Loki!

LOKI *catches the action and reacts.*

> LOKI
>
> Holy shit—the Apostle!

He leaps from the table. JAY *stirs and wakes up suddenly, still half-asleep.*

> JAY
>
> I didn't come in you, I swear . . .

BARTLEBY, *with* BETHANY *in hand, faces off against* RUFUS. LOKI *joins them.*

> LOKI (*to* RUFUS)
>
> What are you doing here?

> BARTLEBY
>
> This one just told me that she's supposed to stop a couple of angels from entering a church.

> LOKI
>
> You think she was talking about us?

> BARTLEBY

No—two other fucking angels! I'd say there was a pretty good chance!

> (*to* RUFUS)

What do you say, Rufus—we're to be liquidated?

> RUFUS

You haven't thought about the consequences of your reentry!

> LOKI

Consequences, schmonsequences.

> BARTLEBY

Guess what? We're going home, regardless of whose pride it may hurt! And no one—not you, and especially not this finite-lifer—is going to impede us!

> RUFUS

It's not a matter of pride, stupid!

> BARTLEBY

Loki—kill the girl!

> LOKI (*beat*)

What are you, high?

> BARTLEBY

Do it!

> LOKI

I can't kill her if she hasn't done anything, you know that.

> BARTLEBY

Fine! I'll kill her myself . . .

A hand lands on Bartleby's shoulder.

> JAY (*oblivious to the situation*)

What the fuck is this shit? I fall asleep for five minutes and everyone takes off? You guys are fucking flat-leavers!

BARTLEBY *turns the knife on him.*

> JAY (*not quite getting it yet*)

We having cake or something?

> BARTLEBY (*to* LOKI)

Shut his mouth!

LOKI *backhands* JAY , *who drops to the floor.* SILENT BOB *grabs* LOKI *and hurls him down the aisle.* RUFUS *grabs Bartleby's knife hand. They struggle.* BETHANY *collapses.*

RUFUS

TUBBY! THE DOOR!

SILENT BOB *drags* LOKI *by the collar to the back door of the car, then opens it.*

LOKI

Wait, man! Can't we talk about this?! Why don't I just get off at the next stop?!?

He throws LOKI *through the door, off the train.*

RUFUS *slams Bartleby's hand against a seat.* BARTLEBY *drops the knife and punches* RUFUS *in the face.* BETHANY *jumps on Bartleby's back, covering his eyes. They careen down the aisle, toward* SILENT BOB *. He pulls* BETHANY *off Bartleby's back and kicks him out the back door, off the train. He quickly slams the door closed and leans against it.*

A PASSENGER—*slumbering in the back of the car until the ruckus started— stares at him.* SILENT BOB *brushes off his coat and thumbs toward the door.*

SILENT BOB

No ticket.

RUFUS *rubs his jaw.* BETHANY *crawls up beside him, breathing heavily.*

BETHANY

I should have known something was wrong when he paid for all the drinks.

INT UNDERGROUND GARAGE—NIGHT

A door is kicked open. LOKI *enters, brushing himself off.* BARTLEBY *follows.*

LOKI

The Apostle is here!

BARTLEBY

I noticed.

LOKI

Then you know who the chick with him was!

BARTLEBY

The Scion, I'd imagine.

LOKI (*in a panic*)

Well, shit, man! Maybe we should rethink this whole thing! I mean, you heard the guy—he said there were consequences! Azrael tells us we're marked! Maybe there's more to this than we thought about!

BARTLEBY *stares into space. His demeanor has suddenly changed.*

BARTLEBY

I was close, you know. So close to just slitting that bitch's throat. And you know how I felt? Righteous. Justified. Eager, even.

LOKI (*beat*)

Are you alright? Your eyes are kinda—

BARTLEBY

My eyes are opened. When that sweet, innocent girl let her mission slip, I had an epiphany. For the first time in all these eons, I get it. See—in the beginning, it was just us and Him. Angels and God. And then He created the humans. Ours was designed to be a life of servitude and worship and adoration. But He gave them more than He ever gave us. He gave them a choice. They choose to acknowledge God, or choose to ignore Him. All this time we've been down here, I've felt the absence of the Divine Presence. And it's pained me . . . as I'm sure it must have pained you. And why? Because of the way He made us. Had we been given free will, we could ignore the pain—like they do. But no—we're servants!

LOKI

Okay. I think one of us needs a little nap.

BARTLEBY

Loki—wake up! The humans have besmirched everything bestowed on them. They were given Paradise; they threw it away. They were given this planet; they destroyed it. They were favored best among all His endeavors; and some of them don't even believe He exists! And in spite of it all, He's shown them infinite fucking patience at every turn.

(*looks at* LOKI)

What about us? I once asked you to lay down the sword because I felt sorry for them. What was the result? Our expulsion from Paradise! WHERE WAS HIS INFINITE FUCKING PATIENCE THEN?!? IT'S NOT FAIR!!

(*smiles*)

We've paid our debt. Don't you think it's time we went home? And to do that, I think we have to dispatch our would-be dispatchers.

LOKI

Wait, wait, wait—kill them?! You're talking about the Last Scion, for Christ's sake! And what about Jay and Bob—I mean, those guys were alright.

BARTLEBY

Don't, my friend. Don't let your sympathies get the best of you. They did me once. Scion or not, she's just a human. And by passing through that archway, our sins are forgiven. No harm, no foul.

LOKI (*shocked*)

My God . . . I've heard a rant like this before . . .

BARTLEBY

What did you say?

LOKI

I've heard a rant like this before.

BARTLEBY

Don't you fucking do that to me . . .

LOKI

You sound like the Morningstar.

BARTLEBY

YOU SHUT YOUR FUCKING MOUTH, SERAPH!

LOKI

You do—you sound like Lucifer. You've fucking lost it, man. You're not talking about going home, Bartleby—you're

talking about fucking war on God! Well, fuck that—I've
already seen what happens to the proud when they take on
the Throne. I'm going back to Wisconsin.

LOKI *turns to leave, but* BARTLEBY *grabs him, slamming him against the wall.*

> **BARTLEBY**
> We're going home, Loki! And no one—not even the Almighty
> Himself—is going to make that otherwise.

BARTLEBY *releases* LOKI *and smiles. He exits.* LOKI *watches him go.*

> **LOKI**
> Shit.

He follows.

EXT CAMP FIRE—NIGHT

*Another newspaper headline regarding "John Doe Jersey" fills the frame. It
is lowered to reveal* JAY, BETHANY, *and* RUFUS *sitting around a makeshift
fire in the middle of nowhere.* JAY *rolls a joint.* SILENT BOB *reads the paper.*

> **BETHANY**
> I don't understand why we couldn't stay on the train. You
> threw those guys off.

> **RUFUS**
> A very basic strategy—if your enemies know where you are,
> then don't be there.

> **BETHANY**
> And what's with that? Why are we enemies?

> **RUFUS**
> I know I'd perceive the person sent to kill me as my enemy.

> **BETHANY**
> What does that mean? I wasn't asked to kill anybody—just
> stop them from going into that church.

> **RUFUS**
> And how were you going to do that? Show them your titties?

> **BETHANY**
> I've never killed anything before in my life!

JAY

I'll do it.

RUFUS

Shut the fuck up, little man—you couldn't kill a pint of ice cream, let alone an angel.

JAY

Fuck you—I can kill an angel as good as the next guy.

RUFUS (*ignoring* JAY; *to* BETHANY)

Killing an angel's a two-step process—first you have to cut off their wings, which then makes them human. From that point on, it's the same as killing anyone else—head or heart, take your pick.

BETHANY

You say it as if it's easy.

RUFUS

The question may be moot. When you were visited by the Metatron, did you get this feeling . . . Down *there*?

BETHANY

Oh my God—yes! It felt like someone . . .

RUFUS

Caressed your hoo-ha, right? That's what's called the Presence. It's an aura angels have—residue from being in the presence of God. When it's absorbed into a human's bloodstream—usually by smell—it goes right to their erogenous zones. It's why angels used to get laid so much back in the days before God took away their gear. But you didn't feel that around Bartleby and Loki, did you?

BETHANY

No. I mean, I felt something for Bartleby . . .

RUFUS

That was probably the booze.

JAY

Aw, you wanted to fuck that guy? What about me?

BETHANY *rolls her eyes.*

RUFUS

If you didn't get that feeling around them, my guess is
someone's protecting Bartleby and Loki; shielding them from
detection. Someone with juice. You should've felt them. But
I'm more surprised they didn't feel *you*.

JAY

Tell me about it. If she gave me half a chance, I'd feel her,
alright . . .

BETHANY

Shut up.
                                   (*to* RUFUS)
What does that mean? I'm tired of all this cryptic bullshit. I'm
physically and psychologically exhausted, Rufus, and I'm
about to kick back and welcome the end of existence with
open arms, unless you come clean—right now! Why me? Out
of everyone on the whole goddamned planet, why was I
tapped?

RUFUS *looks at her. He shrugs.*

RUFUS

Family ties.

JAY

That show's funny as hell, man—Alex P. Keaton like a
motherfucker . . .

RUFUS *backhands* JAY. SILENT BOB *holds* JAY *back, while* RUFUS *addresses*
BETHANY.

RUFUS

Imagine you're a twelve-year-old boy, and one day you're
told you're God's only Son. And more than that—you're God.
How long do you think it'd take you to come to grips with
something that huge? Maybe, say . . . eighteen years?
                                   (*beat*)
In the Bible, Jesus suddenly goes from age twelve to thirty.
Now that's some poor storytelling. Where are the volumes of
text dealing with the missing eighteen years? I'll tell you

where. It was offered up as a sacrifice to the god of
ecumenical politics.

BETHANY (*laughs*)

You make it sound like there's some conspiracy to cover up
"the truth about Christ."

RUFUS *offers her a serious look. He then stands and starts circling the fire.*

RUFUS

In upper Egypt, there's this little place called Nag Hammadi.
And in 1945, an Arab peasant dug up an earthenware jar,
inside of which were fifty-two Coptic manuscripts, translated
from the original Greek, buried in the ground for sixteen
hundred years. They found the entire Gospel of Thomas in
that jar.

BETHANY

Wait, wait, wait—Matthew, Mark, Luke, and John, Rufus.
There is no Gospel of Thomas in the Bible.

RUFUS

Exactly.

BETHANY

I don't get it.

RUFUS

It's not in the Bible for a reason. Neither are the other books
they found—The Apocryphon of John, The Gospel to the
Egyptians, The Gospel of Truth. All books written by an early
group of Christians called the Gnostics.

BETHANY

Why haven't I heard of these books?

RUFUS

Politics. Early Christianity was made up of all sorts of folks
slung far and wide practicing faiths based on the teachings of
Jesus Christ—whether learned firsthand from the Apostles or
filtered down from their followers. One group of said
Christians were the Gnostics—who believed that Christ came
to *enlighten* us—not save us from sin or make us repent. But
then Bishop Irenaeus comes along in the second century, and

he's not comfortable with all the diversity. So he and his
followers insist there can be only one church, outside of
which there is no salvation. It was the birth of what he called
the *Catholic*—meaning *universal*—church.

BETHANY

Why didn't they just incorporate what these Gnostics
believed? Then there'd be more members—they'd have a
larger, stronger church.

RUFUS

When you're building a religion, you want to establish a firm
line of what is and what isn't, so you can control folks. If you
tell people such and such is a sin, and doing it'll send them to
Hell, you keep the peace. When the Catholic Church decided
to dictate the truth, the Gnostics got knocked out of the box;
regardless of the fact that what they believed was just as
valid as what Irenaeus believed—perhaps even more so. But
centuries later, the manuscripts found at Nag Hammadi
present data that conflicts with the lore the early Catholic
Church had already established as the basis of their religion.
The current Church couldn't refute centuries of dogma, so
they thought it best to let sleeping dogs lie, and the new stuff
never got added. Whole books disregarded, even though they
include accounts of the life of Jesus Christ. And that's one of
the reasons man struggles in his relationship with God—he
has a fundemental lack of comprehension, which isn't even
our fault. We were never given the complete picture. All we
got was a book that holds an extremely biased account of
religious history.

BETHANY

Oh, come on. Any integral material about Christ would give
people a better understanding of the nature of God. Why
would they leave any of it out?

RUFUS

Because it was all closely tied in with His family.

BETHANY

His mother and father?

RUFUS

His brothers and sisters.

BETHANY (*beat*)

Wait, wait, wait—Jesus didn't have any brothers or sisters.
Mary was a virgin.

RUFUS

Mary gave birth to *Christ* without having known a man's
touch—that's true. But she did have a husband. And do you
really think he'd have stayed married to her all those years if
he wasn't getting laid? The nature of God and the Virgin
Birth—those are leaps of faith. But to believe a married
couple never got down . . . ? Well, that's just plain gullibility.

BETHANY

Meaning?

RUFUS

The blood that flows in your veins shares a chromosome or
two at the genetic level with the man you call Jesus.
(*hand on her shoulder*)
Bethany—you are the great-great-great-great-great-great-
great-great-great-great-great-great-great-grand-niece of Jesus
Christ.

*Bethany's jaw drops. Every emotion imaginable races across her face. Her
eyes tear up. Her bottom lip quivers.*

JAY (*takes a hit from his joint*)

So . . . that would make Bethany part black.

BETHANY (*gets up*)

I can't do this anymore . . .

RUFUS (*gets up*)

Where you gonna go, Bethany? Where you gonna run that'll
erase what I just told you, or make it untrue? You know what
I'm saying is right.

BETHANY (*meekly; dazed*)

It's . . . bullshit . . .

                              RUFUS
Bethany . . .
                        (*places arm around her*)
                    BETHANY (*pushes him away; screaming*)
IT'S BULLSHIT!!!

RUFUS , JAY , *and* SILENT BOB *stare—shocked. Bethany's wide-eyed and frantic now. She backs up like a cornered animal, and then dashes into the night.*

SILENT BOB *moves to run after her, but* RUFUS *grabs his arm.*

                              RUFUS
Let her go, man. Give her time.

EXT WOODS—NIGHT

BETHANY *runs through the brush, trees, and thickets—crying, muttering, hysterical.*

EXT LAKESHORE—NIGHT

She emerges by a placid lake, and doesn't stop—running straight into the water and collapsing to her knees. In tears, she screams skyward.

                             BETHANY
WHY?!? WHY ME?!? WHAT THE FUCK DO YOU WANT
WITH ME?!? I FUCKING HATE YOU!!!
                            (*broken*)
I hate you . . .

And there she sits, waist-deep in the water; shattered and alone. Until . . .

                            METATRON
He can't hear you, you know.

BETHANY *looks up.* METATRON *stands atop the water, in the middle of the lake.*

                            METATRON
That's why we needed you.

                            BETHANY
WHY DIDN'T YOU TELL ME?!?

METATRON (*walking toward her*)

Would you have . . . *Could* you have believed me? It was
something you had to come to gradually. Only after
everything you've seen, everything you've heard could you
possibly be able to accept the truth.

BETHANY (*crying*)

I don't want this . . . It's too big . . .

METATRON

That's what Jesus said.

BETHANY *whimpers. She looks to* METATRON.

METATRON

Yes. I had to tell him. And you can imagine how that hurt the
Father—not to be able to tell the Son Himself because one
word from His lips would destroy the boy's frail human
form? So I was forced to deliver the news to a scared child
who wanted nothing more than to play with other children. I
had to tell this little boy that He was God's only Son, and that
it meant a life of persecution and eventual crucifixion at the
hands of the very people He came to enlighten and redeem.
(*helps* BETHANY *up*)
He begged me to take it back—as if I could. He begged me to
make it all untrue. And I'll let you in on something,
Bethany—something I've never told anyone before . . .
(*beat*)
If I had the power, I would have.
(*shrugs*)
It's unfair. It's unfair to ask a child to shoulder that
responsibility. And it's unfair to ask you to do the same now.
I sympathize. I do. I wish I could take it all back.
(*beat*)
But I can't. This is who you are.

BETHANY

I feel like my entire life . . . everything I am . . . has been a lie . . .

METATRON

No, no, no. Knowing what you now know doesn't mean
you're not who you were. You *are* Bethany Sloane—nobody
can take that away from you . . . not even God. All this means
is a redefinition of that identity—the incorporation of this
new data into who you *are*. Be who you've always been . . .
but just be this as well, from time to time.

METATRON *smiles at* BETHANY. *She's calmer now. They walk toward the
shore.*

BETHANY

I guess this means no more cheating on my taxes.

METATRON

Perhaps we should adjourn to someplace a tad more
habitable, and a bit warmer.

INT FOUR STAR RESTAURANT—NIGHT

We're in a posh, classic dining room, where we find BETHANY, RUFUS, JAY,
and SILENT BOB *sitting at an elegant table. All look disoriented, except* JAY,
who continues to smoke his joint. He offers it to SILENT BOB, *who still holds
his newspaper.*

JAY

Fuck—I think this shit just kicked in.

RUFUS

I'm sorry—weren't we just in the woods? What are we doing
here, now?

OC METATRON

Going out in style.

METATRON *joins them, sitting.* RUFUS *is taken aback.*

RUFUS

The Voice!

METATRON (*mimicking his shock*)

The Apostle!

JAY

Now who's *this* motherfucker?

RUFUS

It's the Voice of God—show some respect.

JAY

Oh, the Voice of God? Where's the rest of Him?

METATRON

Funny you should mention that—we're not sure.

RUFUS

What?

METATRON

Come on, Apostle. Didn't it ever occur to you that this
Bartleby/Loki situation was well within the sphere of His
control?

RUFUS

Yes. But then why was she tapped?

METATRON (*sighs*)

You know those constitutionals He likes to take?

BETHANY

Constitutionals?

RUFUS

I think we're beyond euphemisms at this point.
(*to* BETHANY)
God's a Skee-Ball fanatic.

METATRON

Let's not altogether blow some of the mystery that surrounds
Him, alright?
(*to* BETHANY)
Yes—the Lord has quite a fancy for the game. He's been
playing it for years. He assumes a human form once a month
and indulges. Doesn't tell anyone where He's playing; just
goes away for a couple of hours. And from what I
understand, He always gives his free points away to
neighborhood children. Isn't that sweet?

BETHANY

But She hasn't come back from one of those day-trips, is what
you're saying?

METATRON (*to* RUFUS)
"She"? I take it she's met the Muse.
(*to* BETHANY)
No, "She" hasn't. And we've been unable to locate "Her."

RUFUS
Maybe He was killed? Human form does have that
drawback.

METATRON
No—there's a different sort of foul play afoot, children.
Whoever has set the renegade angels on their path and is
keeping them quite well-hidden is also responsible for the
Lord's whereabouts. Were He to be killed in human form,
He'd have immediately returned to Heaven. Somebody knew
enough to keep the body alive, but incapacitate Him in
another fashion. And as omnipotent as we are above, I have
to admit that we're more or less lost without His presence.
We've had our people looking everywhere for Him. And I
tapped her, because I thought we might be able to smoke out
whoever's behind this. But whoever it is has been clever
enough to send some lackeys after you, as opposed to
showing up themselves.

RUFUS
Could it be Lucifer?

METATRON
No, it's not Lucifer. Thankfully they seem oblivious to the
situation in the nether-regions. I know they're not
responsible—at least not Lucifer. If he was, he'd have made
his move by now to conquer Heaven. And I know he's not
responsible for Bartleby and Loki because he'd have just as
much to lose by their return as everyone else.

RUFUS
Then what about the Golgothan and the Triplets?

METATRON
Don't be stupid—demons aren't exclusive to Hell. Anybody
can summon one.

JAY (*excited*)

Yeah?

SILENT BOB *hands* JAY *his newspaper and points.* JAY *reads.*

BETHANY

Then why did you lie to me? You said I was tapped as a test?

METATRON

No, you said that—I just didn't correct you. How do you think you would've taken it if I told you the face of God belonged on the back of a milk carton?

RUFUS

So what do we do now?

METATRON

I say we get drunk, because I'm all out of ideas.

JAY (*off paper*)

Why don't we just ask this guy to close the church?

METATRON

I beg your pardon?

JAY

Here.

(*hands group the paper*)

It's the guy in charge of the church thing.

BETHANY (*reading*)

"Glick's Campaign in Hot Water"? "In the latest step to revitalize the Church under the aegis of the Vatican-sanctioned 'Catholicism—Wow!' campaign, the movement's architect, Cardinal Ignatius Glick, today announced the proposed replacement of the traditional baptismal fonts with wooden tubs more Jacuzzi-like in appearance."

JAY

Maybe we could just ask him to shut down the church. If it's closed on that day, those guys can't get blessed or whatever—right?

METATRON

Good Lord—the little stoner's got a point.

BETHANY

I think Silent Bob had a point. But we could go talk to this guy Glick. I'm sure we could explain the situation somehow, talk him into calling off the rededication . . .

RUFUS

"We"? Are you saying you're back in, Miss "I-Can't-Do-This-Anymore"?

The assembled group awaits a reply. She stares at them for a long beat, then smiles.

BETHANY

I wouldn't want to let the family down, now would I?

METATRON (*off* SILENT BOB)

Well—the prophets finally live up to their titles.

SILENT BOB *shrugs.* JAY *sips his brandy and winces.*

JAY

This sucks, man. Can I get a Shirley Temple?

INT GLICK'S OFFICE—DUSK

BETHANY, RUFUS, JAY, *and* SILENT BOB *watch* CARDINAL GLICK *putt into an overturned glass.*

GLICK

Mass attendance is at an all-time low in this country. And it's not like we're losing them to the Protestants or Baptists—people aren't practicing any denomination at all these days. But if we can sell them some show—let 'em know the Catholic Church has a little panache—we can win them back. Even get some new ones. Fill them pews, people—that's the key. Grab the little ones as well. Hook 'em while they're young.

(*sits at his desk; lights smoke*)

RUFUS

Kind of like the tobacco industry?

GLICK

Oh—if only we had their numbers.

JAY *and* SILENT BOB *adjourn themselves from the group and approach a hat rack, where the Cardinal's cassock and miter hang.* JAY *nudges* SILENT BOB.

> OC BETHANY
>
> We really appreciate you seeing us this late in the day, Your Eminence. My friends and I have been traveling all night in hopes of getting a chance to talk to you about the Saint Michael's rededication ceremony.

> GLICK
>
> You're looking to help out in some way, I take it?

> BETHANY
>
> We'd like you to cancel the ceremony.

> GLICK (*beat*)
>
> I beg your pardon?

SILENT BOB *stands alone by the hat rack.* JAY *leaps into the frame, cassock tied around his shoulder like a cape. He strikes a Superman pose.*

> BETHANY
>
> There's going to be a world of trouble if tomorrow's ceremony goes forward as planned.

> GLICK
>
> What is this—a threat? Are you planning some sort of demonstration?
>
> (*pause*)
>
> Are you pro-choice?

> BETHANY
>
> No, the trouble's not from us. It's from these renegade angels who've been stuck on earth since the plagues . . .

RUFUS *side-kicks* BETHANY, *nonchalantly but firmly.*

> BETHANY
>
> Uh . . . these guys who *think* they're renegade angels.

> RUFUS
>
> See padre, it goes down like this—these guys think that by passing through that archway, they can go straight to Heaven.

SILENT BOB *watches as the miter appears slowly from behind the partition, resembling a shark fin. It "swims" to and fro, menacingly.* SILENT BOB *shakes his head.*

> GLICK
>
> And you want me to call off the ceremony . . . for that?

> BETHANY
>
> Well, they're very passionate about it. Dangerously so. They could turn violent if they walk through that arch and nothing happens.

> RUFUS
>
> These guys could blow, and if they do, they're going to take some people with them. So please—call this thing off.

> GLICK (*beat*)
>
> Who sent you? Someone from the Council of Churches, right? Somebody's upset that we're getting so much publicity? Who was it? Rabbi Sloss?

> RUFUS
>
> We were sent by Him who is called I Am!

> GLICK
>
> Cute.
>
> (*standing*)
>
> Playtime with the Cardinal is over.

> RUFUS (*to* BETHANY)
>
> Worked for Moses.

> BETHANY
>
> Stay out of this.
>
> (*to* GLICK)
>
> Your Eminence, it's not a joke. These guys are an accident waiting to happen. And if the rededication ceremony goes on as planned . . .

> GLICK
>
> . . . then these loonies will show up and go nuts, thus endangering the lives of all assembled, including the Governor, the press, me, the leaders of the Council of Churches. Heck, let's not stop there, maybe even God Himself.

BETHANY

You can't say "Himself"; it could be a woman.

GLICK

Your passion for all topics insignificant, including the gender
of our Almighty Lord, tests my patience, people. Now I'm a
very important man with very important matters that
demand my attention, so if you'll please—

RUFUS

I'm telling you, man, this ceremony is a big mistake.

GLICK

The Catholic Church does not make mistakes.

RUFUS

Please! What about the Church's silent consent to the slave trade?

BETHANY

And its platform of noninvolvement during the Holocaust?

GLICK (*beat*)

Alright—mistakes were made. But one can hardly hold the
current incarnation of Holy Mother Church responsible for
oversights of old. Now I've indulged you for more time than I
should have. Please go.

BETHANY

But tomorrow . . .

GLICK (*losing it*)

Tomorrow goes off without a hitch! Do I make myself clear?! I
did not labor two years and exhaust every ounce of my being
to insure that this ceremony be a cornerstone in the most
important liturgical event since Vatican Two just to cancel it at
the zero hour at the insistence of a wandering band of
pranksters who've targeted me as the focus of their evening's
merriment! This occasion is important for the congregation of
this parish, for the massive crowds coming for the plenary
indulgence, for me, for His Holiness the Pope, and—most
importantly—for the "Catholicism—Wow!" campaign! And
neither you, nor any other influence short of the hand of God . . .

(*glares at* BETHANY)

... *HIM*-self is going to keep this thing from going off without a hitch!

He violently grabs the miter/shark fin "swimming" behind the partition.

>   GLICK
> AND TAKE OFF MY GODDAMN HAT!!!

JAY *slowly peeks over the partition.*

EXT TURNPIKE—EARLY MORNING

Amidst very little traffic, two figures emerge from the shadows on the Pennsylvania side. BARTLEBY *and* LOKI *step purposefully past the green sign that welcomes motorists to New Jersey.*

INT BAR—DAWN

The place is empty, except for BETHANY, RUFUS , JAY, *and* SILENT BOB *and* BARTENDER.

>   BETHANY
> I can see the headlines now . . . if there were going to be any—
> "Existence Erased, Thanks to Some Prick in a Scarlet Cape."

>   JAY
> Don't worry, man—we evened the score.
>   (*to* SILENT BOB)
> Hand it over, Silent Bob.

SILENT BOB *pulls a golf club from out of his coat.*

>   BETHANY
> We're going straight to Hell, I know it.

>   RUFUS
> You stole the Cardinal's driver?

>   JAY
> Why's everyone so scared? He's just another guy in a dress.
> And this is what he gets for messing with our girlfriend—the
> cross-dressing fuck.

>   BETHANY
> That's sort of sweet. Thanks, guys.

(*to* RUFUS)
So what do we do now—about Bartleby and Loki?

RUFUS
I guess we're going to have to try to kill them.

BETHANY
But you said they couldn't be killed.

OC VOICE
Correction: they *won't* be killed.

The gang turns to see AZRAEL *sitting at the bar.*

AZRAEL
And just to insure that, we're all going to sit tight, right here,
until those two idiots pass through that arch.

JAY
Hey . . . !

BETHANY
He wasn't talking about you two.

OC VOICE
There's only one idiot here, Azrael . . .

BETHANY *and* RUFUS *react, as does the very surprised* AZRAEL.

SERENDIPITY *stands in the doorway.*

SERENDIPITY
And I'm looking right at him.

AZRAEL
The Muse. Just in time to join us for a drink.

BARTENDER (*suddenly noticing* AZRAEL)
Hey. Where'd you come from?

AZRAEL
Me? Nothingness. And that's where I'm returning to in
approximately . . .
(*checks watch*)
. . . one hour.

BARTENDER
Alright, Plato—sounds like you've had enough already. Let's go.

AZRAEL

Come on, barkeep—just one drink for the road. Then I'm
gone.

SERENDIPITY *joins* BETHANY *and* RUFUS . *She whispers.*

SERENDIPITY

I was trying to find you—to tell you I'd figured out who was
behind all this.

RUFUS

Is that who I think it is?

SERENDIPITY

None other than.

BETHANY

Who is it?

SERENDIPITY

That's my worst suspicions confirmed.

The BARTENDER *relents.*

BARTENDER

Alright—one drink. Then you're gone.

AZRAEL

Gimme a Holy Bartender.

BARTENDER

Never heard of it.

AZRAEL (*to the group*)

He doesn't know how to make a Holy Bartender. You
know—don't you, Muse?

SERENDIPITY

Azrael . . . don't.

AZRAEL (*ignoring her*)

Anybody? Well—*I* know how to make a Holy Bartender.

AZRAEL *pulls an Uzi from his coat and blows a dozen holes in the* BARTENDER.
The STYGIAN TRIPLETS *burst through the floor and everyone jumps to their
feet.*

AZRAEL

Get it?

SERENDIPITY

Sweet Jesus, Azrael—why?!?

RUFUS (*rushing him*)

C'mon, demon—let's see you try that shit on someone who's already dead!

The STYGIAN TRIPLETS *cross their sticks in front of* RUFUS *to block him as* AZRAEL *trains his Uzi on* BETHANY.

AZRAEL

Oh, Apostle—you maintain that kind of an attitude and you and the barkeep won't be the only corpses in the room—the Christ-Bitch will join you.

SERENDIPITY

Are you really that stupid?! You *do* know what's going to happen if those two jerks enter that church?!

AZRAEL

I'm actually counting on it! And if my calculations are correct, the pawns are moving into checkmate as we speak.

Everyone stares at AZRAEL, *with the exception of* JAY, *who suddenly laughs.*

JAY

I get it! Holy Bartender! That's a great one!

EXT SAINT MICHAEL'S CHURCH—MORNING

A formidable crowd of parishioners surrounds a small stage, ten yards from the front of the church. Banners hang everywhere, heralding "Catholicism— Wow!" as well as the Centennial of Saint Michael's. The media eats it up.

Cardinal GLICK *stands at the podium, all smiles. He's in mid-speech.*

GLICK

. . . I'd also like to acknowledge this great state's Governor, Elizabeth Dalton, for coming out this morning. True, she's a Protestant—but we won't hold that against her.

(*crowd laughs*)

Now, let me just give you a bit of history on this particular hundred years young House of God . . .

OC BARTLEBY

"God's House"? God doesn't live here anymore.

BARTLEBY *pushes his way through the crowd, sheepishly followed by* LOKI.

BARTLEBY

He's grown weary of your superficial faith. He's turned a deaf ear to your lip-service prayers. He has abandoned you— His favorites—to the whim of judgment. Hypocrites and charlatans—prepare to taste God's wrath!

LOKI (*whispering*)

Maybe we should just leave.

BARTLEBY

You wanted your body count, you got it. This lot is rife with sin. We'll judge them all!

GLICK *grabs a* COP *from the crowd and pushes him toward the pair.*

GLICK

These are the two I was warned about, Officer McGhee. Please assist them off the church grounds.

The COP *grabs Bartleby's arm.*

COP

Alright, mouthpiece, let's leave the nice Cardinal alone and go for a ride . . .

BARTLEBY *grabs the cop's hand.*

BARTLEBY

Mister McGhee, don't make me angry. You wouldn't like me when I'm angry.

COP

Is that so? Well, let's just . . .

BARTLEBY *throws his other hand forward and twists the Cop's head around in one brisk motion. Loki's eyes bug out. The crowd takes flight.*

BARTLEBY (*releasing dead* COP)

Ladies and gentlemen—you have been judged as guilty of violations against our Almighty God. And this very day—I assure you—you will all pay for your trespasses . . . in blood.

(*to* LOKI)

Wings. Now.

LOKI

I'm feeling a little exposed here . . .

BARTLEBY

DO IT!

INT BAR—LATER

AZRAEL *still hosts his captive audience, Uzi trained on the mortals. The* STYGIAN TRIPLETS *surround them, brandishing their sticks.*

BETHANY (*to* SERENDIPITY)

So he's a muse too?

SERENDIPITY

Former muse. He was kicked out.

AZRAEL

Oh, by all means tell them, Serendipity. Tell them how I was slighted by the Almighty.

SERENDIPITY

You got what you deserved, you yellow shithead.

AZRAEL

Ever the fucking apple polisher. I'd hoped that when you left Paradise, you did it finally because you couldn't tolerate the injustice that was visited upon your own brother.

BETHANY

He's your brother?!

SERENDIPITY

Not technically. We were created at the same time.

AZRAEL

To complement one another. Isn't that sweet?

BETHANY

So what happened?

AZRAEL

Yes—what. Lucifer got restless. He just had to start his little
war for the throne. Heaven became divided into two factions
—the faithful and the renegades. The ethereal planes were
chaotic with battle, angel against angel. And when it was all
over, God cast the rebels into perdition.

SERENDIPITY

But Azrael refused to fight. He wouldn't ally himself to God
or Lucifer. He remained in the middle, waiting to see who
came out victorious.

JAY

What are you—some kind of fucking chicken?!

AZRAEL

No—I was an artist, stupid! I was inspiration! A muse has no
place in battle! My job was to create—period!

SERENDIPITY

So after the fallen were banished to Hell, God turned on those
that wouldn't fight, and my brother here was sent down with
the demons. Something he considers a grave injustice.

AZRAEL

Oh, come on. Don't tell me that you never questioned the
judgment, Serendipity? You don't think the Almighty acted a
little too rashly?

SERENDIPITY

You've been waiting for millions of years to ask me that,
haven't you? It's been on your mind since the moment you
fell. It's been gnawing at you this long.

AZRAEL

Well?

SERENDIPITY

No—it never bothered me, and I'll tell you why: you stood
behind your office, you prick. So you were an artist—big
deal! Elvis was an artist, but that didn't stop him from joining
the service in time of war. That's why he's the King . . . and
you're a schmuck.

BETHANY

So all this is about revenge?! You're going to unmake
existence because you have a grudge against God?!

AZRAEL

After the first million years—no. Revenge was the farthest
thing from my mind. Self-preservation became the only
necessity.

RUFUS

Man, speak English.

AZRAEL

Escape, you half-wit. Escape from Hell became my all-
consuming reason. So I studied the religions and waited for
my opportunity to present itself; which it finally did . . . in
Catholicism, in the form of the plenary indulgence. But I
couldn't exercise it—demons can't become human. No—we
can't transubstantiate . . . but angels *can*.

BETHANY

Bartleby and Loki.

AZRAEL

After that, it was a simple matter or waiting for a church to
celebrate their centennial, and when that finally happened,
applying some of the old inspiration tactics: I sent the pair an
article laced with ideas. An incantation I picked up in the Pit
kept them cloaked and off Heaven's radars, and aside from
the Triplets and the Gologothan, no soul in Hell had a clue as
to what was going on.
                              (*smiles*)
Won't proud Lucifer weep when he realizes I triumphed over
the Power in a way he never dared or dreamed.
                              (*shakes it off*)
But no plan, no matter how intricate, could succeed if the
Almighty was in the realm of the quick. So I dispatched Him
in a fairly ingenious fashion.

SERENDIPITY

How? That's the only thing I couldn't figure out.

AZRAEL

Oh no. I've seen way too many Bond movies to know that
you never reveal all the details of your plan—no matter how
close you may think you are to winning.
                                 (*gets up*)
The only X-Factor was the involvement of the Last Scion. I'm
amazed that someone up there would have the balls to make
a move without the Lord's say-so. Believe me—I sweated
when you stumbled upon my boys on that train. But alas,
here you are—powerless to stop the inevitable.

BETHANY

Look, asshole—I don't know if anyone explained the rules to
you, but if you succeed, *everything* gets blinked out of
existence—even you.

AZRAEL (*beat*)

Human, have you ever been to Hell? I think not. Do you
know that once Hell was nothing more than the absence of
God? And if you'd ever been in His presence, then you'd
realize that's punishment enough. But then your kind came
along—and made it so much worse.

BETHANY

Humans aren't capable of one hundredth the evil a shitbag
demon like you is.

BETHANY *spits in Azrael's face. He slowly wipes it off.*

AZRAEL

Evil is an abstract! It's a human construct! But true to his
irresponsible nature, man won't own up to being its engineer,
so he blames his dark deeds on my ilk. But his selfishness is
limitless, and it's not enough for him to shadow his own
existence. No—he turned Hell into a suffering pit—fire,
wailing, darkness, the kind of place anyone would do
anything to get out of. And why? Because he lacks the ability
to forgive himself. It is beyond your abilities to simply make
personal recompense for the sins you commit. No—you
choose rather to create a psychodrama and dwell in a
foundless belief that God could never forgive your "grievous

offenses." So you bring your guilt and inner-decay with you to Hell—where the horrid imaginations of so many gluttons-for-punishment gave birth to the sickness that has infected the abyss since the first one of your kind arrived there, begging to be "punished." And in doing so, they've trans-formed the cold and solitude to pain and misery. I've spent eons privy to the flames, inhaling the decay, hearing the wail of the damned. I know what effect such horrors have on the delicate psyche of an angelic being!

> (beat)

Would you like to glimpse pain eternal? Look . . .

AZRAEL *places his hand over Bethany's eyes. For about ten seconds, we see some of the most fucked-up and disturbing imagery that can be crammed into 240 frames of film.*

AZRAEL *pulls his hand away.* BETHANY *is fried, convulsing uncontrollably.*

> AZRAEL

I'd rather not exist than go back to that. And if everyone has to go down with me, so be it.

> SERENDIPITY (*holding up* BETHANY)

You're still thinking only about yourself, you fucking child.

> AZRAEL

Now, now, now. Things are getting too tense in here.

> (*grabs remote control*)

Hey! What say we watch a little t.v.?

> JAY

Yo—put on channel nine—*Davey and Goliath*!

A STYGIAN TRIPLET *smacks him with its hockey stick.*

> AZRAEL

Uh . . . I was thinking more along the lines of current events.

On the t.v.—a sweaty and panicked REPORTER *barks into the camera, ob-scuring the chaos behind him. Screams are heard.*

> REPORTER

. . . I repeat—men with huge fucking wings have laid waste to St. Michael's . . . Bullets don't seem to affect them . . . The remaining crowd has dropped to their knees, identifying this as the fabled Apocalypse. I'm not a man of faith, but I'm inclined to agree with them.

SERENDIPITY *looks from the t.v. to* SILENT BOB. SILENT BOB *snaps to attention, looking back at her.* SERENDIPITY *nods to the* golf club. SILENT BOB *shakes his head "no."*

> REPORTER (*looking* OC)
> NO! DON'T COME ANY CLOSER!! PLEASE!! NO!!!

The screen goes snowy. AZRAEL *shuts the t.v. off.*

> AZRAEL
> You see that? And I told them to keep a low profile. I'd be pissed, but in a couple of minutes, it's not going to matter anymore.

AZRAEL *notices the silent exchange between* SERENDIPITY *and* SILENT BOB.

> AZRAEL
> Oh? Now what was that all about?

> SERENDIPITY
> What? Oh, nothing. I had something in my eye.

> AZRAEL
> Now who's the fucking child? What did you tell him, Serendipity—to hit me with the golf club? Are you serious? I'm a fucking demon, and you'd have him assault me with a putter?
> (*to* SILENT BOB)
> Go ahead, then—pick it up. Call it a gift. Come on.

SILENT BOB *picks up the club.* AZRAEL *exposes his chest, stepping back.*

> AZRAEL
> That's it. Now take a shot. Take your best fucking shot. I'm serious, I'm not kidding—take it. C'mon—c'mon, bright boy.
> (*he chuckles*)
> Don't you know anything?

SILENT BOB *swings the club with all his might into Azrael's chest. It caves in, blowing muck and shit everywhere.*

RUFUS, JAY, *and* SERENDIPITY *turn on their captors, grabbing the* STYGIAN
TRIPLETS *by the throats.*

> SERENDIPITY
>
> BETHANY! BLESS THE SINK!

> BETHANY
>
> WHAT?!?

> SERENDIPITY
>
> JUST DO IT!!

BETHANY *leaps over the bar, pushing over the dead* BARTENDER, *and blesses
the melting-ice-filled sink.* SERENDIPITY *leads* RUFUS *and* JAY, *with their*
TRIPLETS *in hand. They submerge them—headfirst—in the sink. Cruddy
steam and muck blows out of the water. The* TRIPLETS *convulse and fall still.*

AZRAEL *clutches at his sucking chest wound, shocked. He looks to* SILENT
BOB, *scared.*

> AZRAEL
>
> But . . . I'm a fucking demon . . .

He drops to his knees, then falls forward, dead. SILENT BOB *is in shock. He
crosses to* JAY *, holding the muck-covered club.* JAY *shakes his head.*

> JAY
>
> The whole fucking world's against us, man. I swear to God.

BETHANY *hops off the bar, joining* SERENDIPITY.

> BETHANY
>
> What just happened?

> SERENDIPITY (*collecting hockey sticks*)
>
> He said it himself . . .
>
> (*as* AZRAEL)
>
> "I'm a fucking demon."
>
> (*as herself*)
>
> You hit a demon with an instrument of God—the pure side's
> always going to do the most damage.

> JAY
>
> Holy shit! Silent Bob's an instrument of God?!

> BETHANY (*catching on*)
>
> No . . . but the driver is, because Glick's the kind of asshole that would bless his own clubs for a better golf game! But the sink . . . ?

> SERENDIPITY
>
> You've got that Divine heritage going for you. Sanctifying is just one of the fringe benefits.

> BETHANY
>
> Remind me to try the water-to-wine trick at my next party.
>
> (*to* JAY)
>
> How far away is this church?

> JAY
>
> Three towns over—about ten miles.

> BETHANY
>
> We've gotta make tracks, people—there isn't much time left. Rufus, grab his gun.

> RUFUS
>
> Ten steps ahead of you. Here . . .
>
> (*tosses her keys*)
>
> Take the bartender's car. He's not going to need it.

RUFUS, JAY, SERENDIPITY, *and* BETHANY *exit.* SILENT BOB *stares down at Azrael's body.* JAY *comes back and yanks him out the door.*

EXT STREET—DAY

CARDINAL GLICK *runs to a pay phone. Sweating and bloody, he looks a mess. He presses "0" and looks around wildly—particularly skyward.*

> GLICK
>
> OPERATOR! SEND MORE POLICE TO SAINT MICHAEL'S PARISH—NOW!! PEOPLE ARE GETTING KILLED BY A LARGE, FLYING THING!

As he speaks, a large shadow falls over him from above. It grows larger, enveloping GLICK. *He drops the receiver, drops to his knees, and screams.*

EXT SAINT MICHAEL'S CHURCH—DAY

BETHANY, JAY , SERENDIPITY, SILENT BOB, *and* RUFUS *stare OC, horrified.*

> ### BETHANY
> Oh my God . . .

Bodies, bodies everywhere—partial, whole, bloody—hanging, burning, up-ended. No one is left standing. It's a scene straight out of Hell.

BETHANY *buries her face in Rufus's chest.*

> ### JAY
> And people wonder why I don't go to church anymore.

> ### RUFUS
> Are we too late?

> ### SERENDIPITY
> To save these poor schmucks, yes. But we still exist.

> ### BETHANY
> Where are they?

> ### RUFUS
> They could already be in the church.

> ### SERENDIPITY
> Which means if they come out, nobody touches them.

> ### JAY
> Are you shitting me? The brother here is going to shred them with his angel-be-good special—ain't you, homey?

> ### SERENDIPITY
> If they've passed through that arch, they come out clean. And if they die, they go straight up—and we know what happens then, right?

> ### JAY
> What if they just kill themselves?

> ### BETHANY
> It's a mortal sin. You die with a mortal sin on your soul and you burn. They're not trying to get to Hell.

> ### JAY
> So then what the fuck are we supposed to do?! Just wait for a solution to fall out of the sky?!

On cue, a body plummets out of the sky and hits the ground before the group, quite like RUFUS *had, way back at the start. This body, however, bursts apart like a body would if dropped from a large height.* JAY *looks at* RUFUS.

> JAY
>
> Friend of yours?

> OC VOICE
>
> No—that was a cardinal.

They all turn to see LOKI, *leaning against a news van, holding a bottle of champagne. His wings are at his feet, cut off—blood-spattered and ashen. He looks exhausted.*

> LOKI
>
> You can't really tell by the face, but the Rosaries are a dead giveaway.

> JAY (*goes for the Uzi*)
>
> IT'S ONE OF THEM!! KILL THAT MOTHERFUCKER!!!

> BETHANY (*struggling to stop him*)
>
> NO . . . !

She slaps the Uzi out of Jay's grip. It clatters to the side.

> BETHANY
>
> Don't you listen?! We can't touch them!

> JAY
>
> I wasn't gonna touch him, I was gonna shoot his ass!

> LOKI (*looking skyward*)
>
> He's been at it for awhile now.

In the distance above—a mere shadow against the sky—something winged soars and stops, releasing what looks like a very panicky human being.

> LOKI
>
> We ran out of parishioners, so he just started picking up anyone off the street and dropping them. You're looking at eons of repression getting purged. If only they'd let us jerk off.
>
> (*backs up*)
>
> Take a step back.

They jump back just as the body hits the ground and explodes. BETHANY
charges at LOKI, *grabbing him and shaking him furiously.*

> BETHANY
> WHY?!? WHAT THE FUCK DO YOU HOPE TO PROVE?!?
> ALL THESE PEOPLE . . . ?!?!

LOKI *slaps* BETHANY *away, nonchalantly.*

> LOKI
> This wasn't my idea, alright? I just wanted to go home.
> *(takes a big champagne swig)*
> We both wanted to go home. But he snapped. When he
> realized who you were and what you were gonna have to do,
> he just lost it.
> *(smiles)*
> The funny thing is, the guy could never stand to see *me* work.
> He said he felt sorry for you people.
> *(looks up)*
> Now look at him.

> JAY
> This guy's drunker than hell.

> SERENDIPITY
> Which means he's human now—his wings have been cut off.
> *(touching Loki's face)*
> Loki . . .

> LOKI *(recognizing her)*
> The Muse! No way! I haven't seen you in a long time! What's
> with the tits?

> SERENDIPITY
> Loki—have you walked through the arch yet? C'mon, tell me!
> Have you gone in and come out through the archway yet?!

> OC BARTLEBY
> No.

BARTLEBY *lands before them, draping his wings at his sides, brushing him-*
self off.

BARTLEBY

We were awaiting your arrival.

SERENDIPITY

Bartleby—listen to me! You can't go through with this! Azrael was just using you! If you go back this way . . .

BARTLEBY *slaps her down.*

BARTLEBY

I've become aware of the repercussions, Muse. I know what I'm doing.

BETHANY *leaps at him, all fists and fury.*

BETHANY

YOU FUCK! YOU SICK, TWISTED FUCK!!!

BARTLEBY *subdues her. He strokes her hair.*

BARTLEBY

Bethany—you of all people should understand what I'm trying to accomplish here. You, too, know what it feels like to be cast aside. But you've only dealt with the pain for a few years. I've dealt with it for millennia. And while you never see your ex-husband or how blissful he is with his new wife . . .
            (*picks up her face and smiles at her*)
. . . And he is . . .
            (*drops her head*)
. . . seeing you people everywhere, every day, on this perfect little world He created for you . . . it's a constant reminder that though my kind came first, your kind was most revered. And while your kind knows forgiveness, we know only regret. A lesson must be taught. All are accountable . . . even God.
            (*steps back*)
Soon a cadre of police will arrive, just in time to kill us as we exit the church. And then this failed experiment called existence will cease to be.

OC LOKI

No!

BARTLEBY *looks behind him.* LOKI *stumbles to his feet.*

> ### LOKI
> I . . . I can't . . . let you do this, Bartleby . . .
> > (*he sways as if drunk*)
>
> I didn't know we . . . we would end existence . . . This has
> gone too far . . . I might have to take you down . . .

> ### BARTLEBY (*to* BETHANY)
> My compatriot. Genocide takes a lot out of him. He's
> weakened. And more importantly, he's now a human being.
> A condition that carries two liabilities: a conscience . . .

BARTLEBY *pulls a knife and guts* LOKI. LOKI *stares at* BARTLEBY *as he dies,*
confused and betrayed.

> ### BARTLEBY
> . . . and a short life span.
> > (*in a whisper; to* LOKI)
>
> Sorry, old friend—but you lost the faith.

BARTLEBY *looks at his fallen friend for a beat, then turns his attention on*
the group. Suddenly, SERENDIPITY *leaps on his back.* RUFUS *and* SILENT
BOB *jump in as well, throwing punches.* SILENT BOB *bites his wing.* JAY *grabs*
BETHANY *and pulls her behind a sound booth.*

> ### BETHANY (*peering out from behind*)
> He's lost it! We're fucked! We're absolutely fucked!

> ### JAY (*pulling off clothes*)
> I hear that shit!

> ### BETHANY
> I can't believe this! We're on the brink of nonexistence and
> God's *still* nowhere to be found! What the fuck kind of deity
> gets kidnapped?!

> ### JAY (*pulling open pants*)
> Amen to that.

> ### BETHANY (*suddenly notices him*)
> What the hell are you doing?!

JAY

I'd say we've got about five minutes left to live; the whole world's going to end. You said you'd fuck me.

BETHANY

Are you a complete lunatic?! Everyone's out there battling that thing and you want to cower back here and jump my bones?! We have to go down fighting!

JAY

No, no, no—no time for that foreplay stuff; just sex.

BETHANY

You're a pig . . . !

JAY

What?! It's all over; nobody's gonna beat that thing! Now we can either lay here all comatose like that John Doe Jersey bastard over there, or we can make with the love.

BETHANY *freezes.*

BETHANY (*finally!*)

What did you say?!

JAY

"Make with the love"? It's a nice way of saying "boning."

BETHANY

No—about John Doe Jersey?

JAY

That guy—the one they won't take off life support—John Doe Jersey. This is where he's at.
    (*points to something in the distance*)
Saint Michael's Hospital—over there.

There, across the street, sits a hospital.

BETHANY (*thinks*)

Where's the nearest boardwalk?

JAY

Look, I ain't got time to win you a prize or something, we gotta get to the fucking . . .

BETHANY

WHERE IS IT?!?

JAY (*scared*)

Asbury Park. About five miles away.

BETHANY

Have you ever been there?!

JAY

Once—with this girl. She wanted to do it on the carousel, but I got sick and started puking.

BETHANY (*grabs his face*)

DO THEY HAVE SKEE-BALL THERE?!?

JAY

Yeah.

BETHANY *kisses* JAY *hard on the lips, jumps up, and looks over the sound booth.*

JAY (*warming up*)

Now that's what I'm talking about.

JAY *tries to make out with* BETHANY *as she gets up.*

RUFUS *and* SERENDIPITY *battle* BARTLEBY, *his wings thrashing about.* SILENT BOB *is getting back on his feet.*

BETHANY

BOB!

SILENT BOB *looks to* BETHANY. *She waves him over and bends back down to* JAY, *who half-closes his eyes and puckers his lips.* BETHANY *pinches his lips together and raises* JAY *to his feet, just as* SILENT BOB *arrives.*

BETHANY

Whatever you do—stall Bartleby from going into that church!

(*to* SILENT BOB)

Bob—come with me!

(*they exit*)

JAY (*calling after them*)

How the hell am I supposed to do that?!

OC BETHANY

Think of something!

JAY *(calling off)*
I already did, but it takes two of us!

EXT SAINT MICHAEL'S HOSPITAL—DAY

BETHANY *and* SILENT BOB *rush in against a throng of people rushing out, screaming.*

P.A. VOICE-OVER
I REPEAT! THIS IS NOT A DRILL! THIS *IS* THE APOCALYPSE! PLEASE EXIT THE HOSPITAL IN AN ORDERLY FASHION! THANK YOU!

INT RECEPTION DESK

Nobody's there. BETHANY *leaps over the desk and starts banging keys on the computer.* SILENT BOB *ducks screaming passerby.* BETHANY *snaps back up.*

BETHANY
Fifth floor! ICU! Let's go!

EXT SAINT MICHAEL'S CHURCH—DAY

BARTLEBY *shakes* RUFUS *off and grabs* SERENDIPITY *by the throat.*

JAY *steps up to the Uzi, grabs it, and clicks off the safety. He trains it on* BARTLEBY.

JAY
HEY! BIG BIRD!!

BARTLEBY *looks up from choking* SERENDIPITY.

JAY
READY FOR THE COUNTING GAME?! COUNT THE SHELLS!!

SERENDIPITY
NO!!!

BARTLEBY *throws* SERENDIPITY *to the side and ducks, spreading his wings out to their full span.*

SLO-MO: JAY *fires, Uzi blasting.*

SLO-MO: Bartleby's wings shred into feathers and bone fragment.

SLO-MO: SERENDIPITY *and* RUFUS *race toward* JAY.

SLO-MO: The last bit of wing left on Bartleby's back falls to the ground.

JAY *drops the Uzi, just as* SERENDIPITY *and* RUFUS *reach him.*

> JAY
>
> No more bu-wets.

RUFUS *looks at* JAY *ruefully and slaps his head.*

> JAY
>
> Now what the fuck would you do that for?!

> SERENDIPITY
>
> Angels have to cut their wings off to become human.

> RUFUS
>
> You just did him a favor, stupid.

BARTLEBY *lifts himself up. He looks around. He reaches back to where his wings were and dips his fingers into the blood. He looks at it and laughs.*

INT SAINT MICHAEL'S ICU UNIT

The OLD MAN—*the one from the verrrry beginning (remember him?) lies in the intensive care ward, hooked up to all types of machines.*

BETHANY *and* SILENT BOB *look at him through the glass, then to each other.*

> BETHANY
>
> I'll do it.

> OC NO-MAN
>
> No one . . . touches the God-husk!

NO-MAN *the Golgothan stands at the other end of the ward hallway.*

BETHANY *and* SILENT BOB *look at each other. They both nod, understanding what has to happen.* BETHANY *kisses* SILENT BOB *hard on the lips.*

> BETHANY
>
> Stall him.

BETHANY *tears into the room with John Doe Jersey.*

NO-MAN *begins lumbering toward* SILENT BOB. SILENT BOB *pulls out the small can of air freshener. He tries spraying it, but it's empty. He tosses the can, and notices a small oxygen tank. He blesses himself, lifts the tank over his head, bellows a war cry, and charges at* NO-MAN, *full speed.*

BETHANY *looks down at the lifeless Old Man.*

> BETHANY
> I hope you're the Skee-Ball type.

She yanks the cords from the wall and from the Old Man's body. Beeping-warnings go off and the Old Man's body convulses.

SILENT BOB *charges toward* NO-MAN. NO-MAN *charges right back.*

EXT SAINT MICHAEL'S CHURCH—DAY

BARTLEBY *looks to* SERENDIPITY, RUFUS , *and* JAY . *Then, he bolts toward the church doors, with the group in hot pursuit.*

INT SAINT MICHAEL'S ICU UNIT

BETHANY *looks on nervously as the Old Man's body thrashes.*

SILENT BOB *charges closer to* NO-MAN.

Suddenly, the convulsing of the Old Man's body stops. A smile crosses his face. And out of nowhere—HUGE FUCKING LIGHT erupts from his chest, shooting through the ceiling. One strand branching off to touch . . .

NO-MAN *the Golgothan. Struck by a beam, it screams and morphs into a pile of flowers.*

SILENT BOB *sees this and stops dead in his tracks, staring at it.*

BETHANY *climbs to her feet and looks into the bed. There's no sign of the light. She quickly turns to exit and is lanced with a hockey stick through her stomach.*

A badly burned, half-decomposed STYGIAN TRIPLET *pushes the blade into* BETHANY.

SILENT BOB *rounds the doorway (oxygen tank still in hand) and sees the* TRIPLET. *He grabs the kid in a headlock and jams the oxygen tank nozzle into his mouth, turning the release valve. The Triplet's head starts inflating like a balloon.* SILENT BOB *lights a cigarette, takes a drag, and then uses the lit smoke to "pop" the Triplet's inflated head. He releases the body and takes another drag from his smoke, his eyes falling on something OC on the floor. Suddenly, his expression goes pale.*

EXT SAINT MICHAEL'S CHURCH—DAY

BARTLEBY *storms across the pavement, racing for the church doors, which he reaches and flings open. HUGE FUCKING LIGHT blinds him, and he drops to his knees, shielding his eyes. Cowering, he looks up to see . . .*

METATRON *standing beside a* WOMAN *in the doorway.*

METATRON
Oh Bartleby . . . was Wisconsin really that bad?

SERENDIPITY *and* RUFUS *drop to their knees and bow.* JAY *looks at them.*

JAY
Now what the hell's going on?! Who's the broad?!

RUFUS (*pulling at Jay's cuff*)
Bow down, stupid!

The WOMAN *stares at* BARTLEBY. *She lays Her hand on his shoulder, helping him to his feet. He stands in frightened awe. She embraces him. He weeps, joyfully. She then steps back and looks at Metatron, who nods and addresses* JAY, RUFUS, *and* SERENDIPITY.

METATRON
Anyone who isn't dead or from another plane of existence would do well to cover their ears right about now.

JAY
What the fuck . . . ?

SERENDIPITY *and* RUFUS *tackle* JAY *and hug his head, covering his ears tightly.*

The WOMAN *turns back to* BARTLEBY. *Her expression hardens. His eyes widen, and then he nods in understanding. He manages a half-smile.*

BARTLEBY

Thank you.

The WOMAN *opens her mouth and emits a deafeningly cacophonous noise. It remains one long note that builds in intensity.*

Bartleby's head explodes, as does his chest through his armor. His body drops to its knees and falls forward. The WOMAN *closes Her mouth and the noise stops.* METATRON *notices Bartleby's blood on his jacket.*

METATRON (*off mess; pissed*)

It never ends!

He grabs a piece of the Woman's gown, spits on it, and begins furiously rubbing at the stain on his jacket. He then thinks better of it, and lets the gown go.

RUFUS *and* SERENDIPITY *look up, releasing* JAY. *They drop to their bowing positions.* JAY *'s in a panic. The* WOMAN *approaches him.*

JAY

What the fuck is this shit?!

(*to* WOMAN)

Who the fuck are you, lady?!

(*to* RUFUS *and* SERENDIPITY)

Why the fuck did you hug my head?!

METATRON (*to* WOMAN)

Quite a little mouth on him, isn't there?

The WOMAN *nods.*

JAY

What the fuck is this—*The Piano?* Why ain't this broad talking?!

METATRON

Young man, I believe the answers you seek lie within my companion's eyes.

JAY

What the fuck does that mean?! Has everyone just gone fucking nuts?! What the fuck happened to that guy's head?! I want some . . .

The WOMAN *stands before* JAY *and looks him in the eyes.* JAY *freezes. His expression softens. The* WOMAN *slowly smiles at him, leans forward, and kisses his cheek. She exits, leaving* JAY *standing there, speechless. He then passes out, collapsing as* SERENDIPITY *and* RUFUS *rise to their feet.*

> SERENDIPITY

Where *was* She?!

> METATRON

Imprisoned in a body. Bethany figured it all out. She's a clever girl, that one.
> (*watching OC*)

Hang on a minute.

The WOMAN *surveys the mess outside the church, as well as the fallen* LOKI. *Her face fills with dismay, and then softens. She smiles, and the exterior of the church is suddenly cleaned up—entirely spotless, with no bodies, blood, or mayhem in evidence.*

SERENDIPITY, RUFUS, *and* METATRON *smile.*

> METATRON (*to* RUFUS)

Are you ready to go back, Apostle?

> RUFUS (*getting up*)

You ready to make some of those changes I've been talking about?

> METATRON

We'll see.
> (*to Serendipity*)

Muse, seeing as how you just *had* to get involved, you're welcome to return with us as well.

> SERENDIPITY

Only if She asks me nicely.

> METATRON

Have fun in the titty clubs.

> SERENDIPITY

Just kidding. Sheesh! First I gotta say goodbye to Bethany— where is she?

SILENT BOB *joins them, eyes glassy, carrying the lifeless* BETHANY. *He gingerly places her on the ground.*

RUFUS

Oh no . . .

SERENDIPITY

Metatron . . . is she . . . ?

METATRON

I'm afraid so. One of the drawbacks to being a martyr is that you have to die. But no matter—all is being taken care of.

SERENDIPITY

How so?

METATRON

Wax on, wax off.

(points OC)

The WOMAN *rolls up Her sleeves and slaps Her palms together—Mister Miyagi style—and rubs them furiously. She places both hands over Bethany's wound and presses down.* BETHANY *snaps her eyes open and jolts forward, coughing.*

BETHANY

But how . . . ! I was . . . ! How did I . . . ?!

METATRON

She can rebuild you. She has the technology. She can make you better, stronger, faster.

BETHANY *looks at the* WOMAN. *The* WOMAN *smiles and heads off. She sniffs some nearby flowers.*

BETHANY

That's . . . ?

METATRON

A very relieved deity. You did well, little girl. I knew you'd come around—your kind always does. So you'd better take good care of yourself. We're going to need you down the road.

BETHANY

I know. I'm the Last Scion.

METATRON

You're half-right—you *were* the Last Scion.
(METATRON *pats her stomach*)
Now *this* . . . is the Last Scion.

BETHANY (*beat*)

I'm . . . pregnant?!?

METATRON

Can't put anything past you. Take care of that parcel for us—
She has a world of work ahead of her.

BETHANY *looks at her stomach, then follows after the* WOMAN. *She catches up to Her on the church steps and taps Her on the shoulder. The* WOMAN *turns and faces* BETHANY.

BETHANY

Um . . . thank You, for . . . I don't know . . . everything.

The WOMAN *smiles.*

BETHANY

There's a million things I wish I could ask, most of it all
questioning what I'm sure is Your great plan, and that would
be really arrogant of me, I know. But there is one I need to
ask, and I'm sure You get it all the time, but how many
oportunities like this will I ever get . . .
(*inhales and exhales*)
Why are we here?

The WOMAN *stares at her for a long beat. Then . . .*

WOMAN

I have one word for you; just one.
(*She leans forward*)
Plastics.

The WOMAN *smiles, beeps Bethany's nose, and heads into the church, followed by* METATRON.

METATRON

Didn't I tell you She was funny?

SERENDIPITY *joins* BETHANY.

SERENDIPITY

You know, She's never even said anything to me. She must really like you.

BETHANY

That's a plus.

SERENDIPITY (*shakes Bethanyís hand*)

I really enjoyed meeting you. It was an honor.

SERENDIPITY *hugs* BETHANY. JAY *makes the "rug-munching" face to* SILENT BOB. SILENT BOB *rolls his eyes.*

SERENDIPITY

You did so well!

(*skipping away*)

I told you She was a woman.

SERENDIPITY *catches up with the* WOMAN *and* METATRON, *as* RUFUS *joins* BETHANY.

RUFUS

She's not really a woman. She's not really anything.

BETHANY

No—She's *something*, alright . . .

RUFUS

Crisis of faith over?

BETHANY

I think I'm now burdened with an overabundance.

RUFUS

When it rains, it pours. You saying you believe?

BETHANY

No.

(*beat*)

But I have a really good *idea.*

She smiles at him. He hugs her.

RUFUS

The Man was right about you. Now I'm gonna go home and tell Him so.

> (*to* JAY *and* SILENT BOB)
>
> And if you clean up your language, I might put in a good
> word for you too.

> SILENT BOB
>
> Thanks.

JAY *hits* SILENT BOB *and shakes his head at him.*

RUFUS *heads into the church.*

> RUFUS (*to* BETHANY)
>
> Why don't you name the kid after me?

A cloud of smoke envelops the WOMAN, METATRON, SERENDIPITY, *and*
RUFUS *as the church doors close.*

BETHANY, JAY, *and* SILENT BOB *stand there, looking on.*

> JAY
>
> (*after a long pause*)
>
> You wanna hear something sick? I got half a stock when she
> kissed me.

> BETHANY
>
> Jay!

> JAY
>
> I couldn't help it! The bitch was hot!

> BETHANY
>
> You know—you can't talk to me that way anymore. I'm going
> to be somebody's mother.

> JAY
>
> You're pregnant?!
>
> (*beat*)
>
> You know, pregnant women can have sex up until their third
> trimester.

> BETHANY
>
> I'll keep that in mind.

*We pan up the front of the church, leaving our trio behind, and end on a
shot of the sky—where God is in His (or Her) Heaven, and all is right with
the world.*